HISTORIC TALES
from
PARK COUNTY

HISTORIC TALES

from

PARK COUNTY

PARKED IN THE PAST

Laura Van Dusen

THE
History
PRESS

Published by The History Press
Charleston, SC 29403
www.historypress.net

Copyright © 2013 by Laura Van Dusen
All rights reserved

Front cover, bottom: Already colorful, Como, Colorado, basks in an explosion of golden aspen leaves in early October. *Author photo.*
Back cover, bottom: Colorado & Southern Engine No. 9 waiting to pull out of the Breckenridge station headed for Como in the mid-1930s. *John Hallinan collection.*

First published 2013

Manufactured in the United States

ISBN 978.1.62619.161.7

Library of Congress CIP data applied for.

Dedicated to the Van Dusen future, my grandchildren—Connor, Gianna and Colbin—and to all who hold a piece of Park County in their hearts.

CONTENTS

Contents

ACKNOWLEDGEMENTS

I acknowledge the following for their contributions to this book: Tom Locke, editor of the *Park County Republican and Fairplay Flume*, for offering the opportunity to write the stories for the September 2011 *Flume* Sesquicentennial Special Edition and for proposing a monthly history feature in the paper, which became "Parked in the Past." The feature and Tom's encouragement led to this book.

Christie Wright, nonfiction historical writer and president of the Park County Local History Archives, for digging up information from the Park County archives and for sharing research sources and bits of hard-to-find facts. When I was looking for a publisher, Christie's list of possibilities led to The History Press.

The Park County Local History Archives for its collection of historical documents and photographs from Park County's past.

Colorado Historic Newspapers and its website, www.coloradohistoricnewspapers.org, for its collection of Colorado newspapers dating from the 1860s. It is an invaluable resource in reading Park County history as it happened.

The History Press for taking the chance on a novice author.

I also acknowledge those who shared their knowledge of Park County history: Larry Frank (chapter 4); John Rankin (chapter 7); Michael Anthony, for his description of the Fluhmann Cave (chapter 12); Margaret Coel and Rick Clapham (chapter 13); Chris Andrew and Wendy Stelle (chapter 14); Dee Lyons for showing the location of Benjamin Ratcliff's cabin and grave (chapter 14); Maury Reiber (chapter 15); Arthur Hall (chapter 17); Como residents Ricki Ramstetter and Margaret Barnes for allowing me access to Como High School (chapter 18); Marie Chisholm (chapter 19) and Tom Weirich (chapter 20); those who shared photographs: Jacquelyn Guiraud Miller and Fred Guiraud (chapter 1); David Stearns (chapter 2); Larry Frank (chapter 4); South Park City Museum and Pioneer Press (chapter 6); Margaret Coel, Diana Copsey, Tom Klinger and Bob Schoppe (chapter 13); Christie Wright (chapter 15); Englewood (Colorado) Public Library (chapter 17); and Tom Weirich (chapter 20); and those entities that provided photos from historic collections: Park County Local History Archives, Colorado State Archives, Alaska State Archives.

I acknowledge my family:

My parents, Elmer and Dorothy King, for raising me to believe in myself; my siblings—Jim, Janice and Vicki—for putting up with me; my sons, Seth and Matt, for growing into the honorable men they have become; and especially my husband, Tom Van Dusen, for his support, patience and understanding that writing inspiration often comes in the hours between 10:00 p.m. and 2:00 a.m.

INTRODUCTION

In September 2011, Park County, Colorado, celebrated the sesquicentennial (150th anniversary) of its 1861 founding as one of the seventeen original counties in the then territory of Colorado. To recognize the date, the

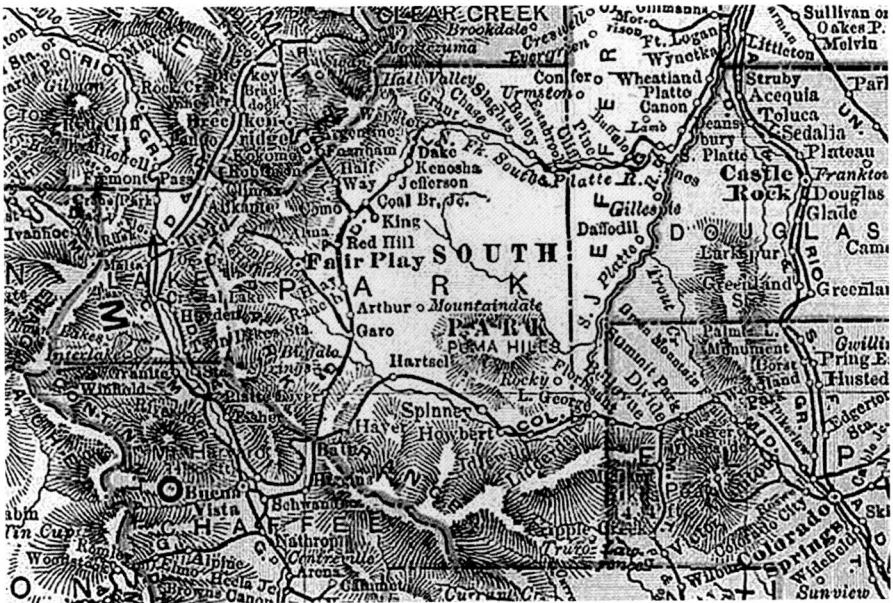

Park County map, 1895. *Park County Local History Archives.*

Park County Republican and Fairplay Flume newspaper (its shortened name, *The Flume*)—through its editor, Tom Locke, and its owner and publisher, Arkansas Valley Publishing—issued a special edition. That edition consisted of four stories I wrote about the 1860s in Park County.

The stories of Benjamin Ratcliff, Marie Guiraud, the Reynolds Gang and Civil War veterans became the basis of a monthly history feature in *The Flume* called "Parked in the Past."

Each of the "Parked in the Past" stories, beginning with the October 28, 2011 *Flume*, focus on a different aspect of the people, places and events of Park County's gold and silver mining, ranching, railroading and early settlement history.

In this book are twenty Park County history stories that first appeared in *The Flume*'s "Parked in the Past" or in the Sesquicentennial Special Edition.

References in this book citing *The Flume* refer to historical issues of the *Fairplay Flume*, dating from 1879, and its rival, the *Park County Republican*, dating from 1912. In 1918, the two newspapers merged into the *Park County Republican and Fairplay Flume*.

1860s

Chapter I

Marie Guiraud

*1860s Pioneer, Mother of Ten,
Widowed at Forty-five, Amassed One of the
Largest Estates in Park County Up to 1909*

Marie Chabreat Guiraud (pronounced "garo") was one of Park County's most prosperous ranchers when she died in June 1909.

Up until October 1875, history recorded little of Guiraud. It was then that husband Adolphe (or Adolph) died, and she was left a widow at the age of forty-five to take care of their modest homestead as best she could and to finish raising the seven surviving progeny of the marriage, ranging in age from twenty-five-year-old Louis to two-year-old Ernest.

As best she could turned out to be quite adequate. In her care, the ranch grew from 640 acres in 1875 with a value of $9,559 (around $200,000 in 2013 dollars) to over 5,000 acres in 1909 valued at $200,000 (around $5,100,000 in 2013 dollars). A rumor circulating after her death told of another $80,000 in gold reportedly found in the basement of her home, stored with the canned goods.

The price of an ounce of gold in 1909 was $18.96; to have $80,000 in gold in 1909, one would have 4,220 ounces. By mid-2013, the value per ounce of gold was $1,388.80, making the 2013 worth for 4,220 ounces nearly $6 million.

Guiraud's estate was said to be "very nearly as great, if not the equal, of the largest estate ever built up in Park County" in her obituary published in the June 11, 1909 *Flume*.

The ranch property was owned by the family until the early 1940s. At the publication of this book, it was owned by the City of Aurora,

Marie Guiraud. *Photo courtesy of Jacquelyn Guiraud Miller and Fred Guiraud.*

Colorado, and known as the Buffalo Peaks Ranch, located near the former town site of Garo between Fairplay and Hartsel on Colorado Highway 9.

Early Years

Marie Chabreat, nineteen, and Louis Adolphe Guiraud, twenty-six, were married in France in March 1848. U.S. census records indicate that their first child, son Louis, was born in France in 1850. Marie faithfully followed Adolphe in his many business endeavors on two continents and in nine locations throughout their twenty-seven years together.

Shortly after the birth of Louis, the Guirauds sailed across the Atlantic to New Orleans, Louisiana. The family didn't stay in New Orleans long; after thirty days, they moved on to Cincinnati, Ohio, where sons Henry, in 1853, and Joseph, in 1857, were born. In the Cincinnati area, Adolphe Guiraud was first a wine importer, later a farmer and then operated a bakery.

In about 1859, Adolphe Guiraud and his brother, who also lived in Cincinnati, decided it was time to move west. The family settled in Leavenworth, Kansas. Adolphe Guiraud operated a public scale, and his wife opened a coffee shop.

Move to Colorado

Also in 1859, farther west in Park County, Colorado, gold was discovered in Tarryall Creek, about two miles above the current site of Como. The towns of Hamilton and Tarryall were founded on opposite sides of the creek.

A friend of Adolphe Guiraud encouraged him to move on to the Colorado gold fields and offered to pay all expenses. Adolphe Guiraud left the family in Kansas in about 1860 and went first to Denver and then to Hamilton, where he opened a store. Adolphe was probably in Hamilton when Park County was named one of the first seventeen counties in the Colorado Territory in November 1861 and Tarryall named the first county seat. The Guirauds' first daughter and fourth child, Mathilda, or "Tillie," was born in Kansas in June 1861, while Adolphe Guiraud was in Colorado.

In 1862, Adolphe Guiraud returned to Leavenworth and moved his family to Colorado, where he homesteaded the 160 acres that later became the heart of the Guiraud Ranch at the future site of Garo. He prospered there, selling hay in Leadville for eighty dollars per ton. Of the ranch's 160 acres, there were 40 to 45 acres planted in wheat, oats, rye, potatoes and vegetables.

On August 27, 1863, the family suffered a tragedy when ten-year-old Henry died in an accident. The family moved to Denver for a fresh start, and Adolphe Guiraud opened a meat market. A year later, the Guirauds were back at the ranch, but soon, they moved to nearby Fairplay, where Adolphe Guiraud operated a grocery store. The grocery failed within months, mainly because the store extended credit to its customers and debts were hard to collect.

The Guirauds went back to the homestead; Adolphe Guiraud expanded operations to include cattle ranching and increased the size of the ranch to 640 acres. Six more children were born in Colorado between 1865 and 1873, including another child named Henry in 1871. Two of the six children born in Colorado died at very young ages.

Perhaps Adolphe Guiraud had found a place to set down deep roots at the Guiraud Ranch, but it was not meant to last. He died in October 1875 at the age of fifty-three.

On Her Own

In the years following her husband's death, Marie Guiraud gradually became one of the most prosperous ranchers in Park County. Her beef cattle sold for the same price as those of her neighbor Sam Hartsel, another successful rancher in the county, for whom the town of Hartsel is named. Guiraud's steers averaged 1,200 pounds, with some weighing in at 1,800 pounds; she was getting four cents per pound (or about one dollar in 2013). She sold not only market beef but also horses. In 1892, she sold two carloads of horses that were shipped to Chicago by train. Although the number of horses and the price per head was not disclosed in *The Flume* article of December 8, it indicates that Guiraud dealt in large quantities of livestock.

In 1879, when Guiraud found out that the under-construction narrow-gauge Denver, South Park & Pacific railroad track would be laid within fifty feet of the ranch, she platted a town across the Middle Fork of the South Platte River from the ranch buildings. The town was called Garo—an

A.S. Turner General Store in Garo, Colorado, in the early 1900s. *Park County Local History Archives, Karen Denison.*

Former Guiraud home in July 2011. *Author photo.*

abbreviated, Americanized version of the family name—because Guiraud had heard the railroad preferred depot towns to have short names.

Guiraud owned one of the first-recorded water rights in the county, dating from 1861, for use of Trout Creek. The rights were put up for sale along with Guiraud's four ranches by her son Ernest, executor of the estate, shortly after Guiraud's death.

Her life was not without additional tragedy. Guiraud buried another son and a daughter during her years running the ranch. Firstborn Louis died in August 1888 at the age of thirty-eight when struck by lightning. Daughter Eugenia Spurlock died on April 21, 1908, at the age of forty-two after an illness of several years.

Guiraud was not afraid to spend money when the situation called for it. When her house burned down in 1906, she immediately had contractors out to the ranch to bid on a "fine, ten-room, one-story building" with dimensions of "54 feet long by 34 feet wide and (costing) over $3,000 when finished," as reported in the May 4, 1906 *Flume*. That price would equal about $80,000 in 2013. *Flume* editions of the following weeks reported that two contractors and the county surveyor were on the scene working on Guiraud's new home.

Guiraud died on June 5, 1909, at the age of seventy-nine. She had been confined to bed for two months before that from paralysis, possibly caused by a stroke. As reported in the January 28, 1910 *Flume*, the six heirs divided $60,000 in cash ($1.538 million in 2013) and the proceeds from the sale of four ranches and the Trout Creek water rights. The rumored $80,000 in gold was not mentioned as part of the estate.

Chapter 2

SAMUEL HARTSEL

*1860s Pioneer Rancher, One of Colorado's First Cattlemen,
Founded Town of Hartsel*

S amuel Hartsel came to Park County in 1860 and left in 1908. During those forty-eight years, he earned success and respect as one of Colorado's first cattlemen.

His operation became "one of the largest and best-stocked cattle ranches of the state," said a story in the 1919 book *The History of Colorado*, volume 4, by Wilbur Fisk Stone.

He also raised sheep and pigs and grew hay, wheat, rye, barley and oats on fifteen thousand acres of owned and leased land. He developed the Hartsel hot springs and built a trading post, wagon shop, sawmill and blacksmith shop at the geographic center of Colorado, where the middle and south forks of the South Platte River meet—the beginnings of the town of Hartsel.

Samuel Hartsel in the late 1880s. *Park County Local History Archives, Samuel Hartsel Collection.*

Hartsel was a handsome man at six feet, one inch tall and slender, with a long, thin nose and short white beard. It was said in a story in the May 1942 edition of the *Colorado Magazine* that he resembled the national icon Uncle Sam.

Business Practices

Hartsel was never in debt.

"It is a noteworthy fact that during his entire business career [Hartsel] has never given a mortgage on a foot of his land nor a chattel mortgage or bill of sale on even one cow or horse; he has bought only what he could pay for," said a story about Hartsel in the 1899 book *Portrait and Biographical Record of the State of Colorado.*

There were some rough winters in the years Hartsel lived in South Park. One was in the early 1880s, when "every spear of vegetation lay four feet deep under the [snow] drifts," said a story in the *Country Gentleman* of November 1925 titled "Sam Hartsel and His Park." (The agricultural magazine was published in Philadelphia from 1831 to 1955.)

It said that when Hartsel saw the herds dying both of starvation and freezing, he and his cowboys "rounded [the cattle] up, drove them eastward out of the mountains and turned them loose." That might have worked, except it was a year of blizzards on the plains as well and dead cattle with Hartsel's brand were found the following spring east of Denver, 150 miles away.

Hartsel, who was retired when the story was written (and had been dead seven years when it was published), was quoted by the author as saying: "I did then what I ought to have had the sense to do years before."

Hartsel fenced off the bottomlands of his ranch, acquired irrigation rights and put up thousands of tons of winter forage from the coarse native meadow grass. He said that the native grass, when irrigated, made excellent hay. Some ranchers had already begun the practice of putting up hay for the winter, and those ranchers were the only ones who pulled through in that blizzard-prone year, the story said.

Early Years

Hartsel was born in Bucks County, Pennsylvania, on November 22, 1834. His cattle career started in about 1849 when he was fifteen. The job was to drive cattle from Ohio to New York. It took four and a half months because Hartsel walked the entire way.

By age twenty-one, he was driving a freight wagon from Fort Leavenworth, Kansas, to locations in what was called the Far West, including Colorado.

He came to South Park in the summer of 1860 for the same reason thousands of others did. He was looking for gold.

When Hartsel arrived at the Tarryall Diggings northwest of present-day Como, Colorado, he was twenty-five years old. The Civil War was a year in the future, and Tarryall and its rival city across Tarryall Creek—Hamilton—together were busy with five thousand prospectors looking for easy pickings of placer gold.

Hartsel spent two unsuccessful months as a prospector, until his provisions ran out. Then he went back to what he knew best: cattle.

Hartsel hired on to herd cattle for two men named Bowers and Warren (their first names were not found), who are credited with the discovery of gold at Tarryall. In 1861, he went out on his own and founded his first ranch. The Pennsylvania Ranch was named after Hartsel's birthplace and was about three miles from Tarryall, possibly to the east along present-day U.S. 285.

At this first ranch, Hartsel's herd consisted of oxen that had brought wagons west. He fattened them up and sold the meat.

In the early years of cattle ranching in South Park, it was thought that cattle and oxen could not survive a South Park winter. Herds were driven to lower elevations in late fall.

One November in the early 1860s, Hartsel couldn't find two of his oxen when the winter drive began, so he left without them. The next April when Hartsel brought the herd back from the lowlands, the missing oxen were waiting at the corral gate. And they were in better shape than the rest of the herd. That's when Hartsel knew for certain that cattle could survive a South Park winter; that discovery gave a boost to the beginnings of cattle ranching in the park.

On average, Hartsel's annual winter losses were "but two or three calves by the wolves," said the December 5, 1874 Colorado Springs *Gazette*.

Unfortunately for the wolves, ranching in Colorado was the beginning of their end. As the predator turned to cattle as easier prey than wildlife, they were gradually eradicated by ranchers. The last wild wolf in Colorado was killed in 1940, according to the Colorado Parks and Wildlife website.

Hartsel Ranch Begins

In 1862, Hartsel moved his cattle operation. He homesteaded 160 acres near a spot that would later become the town of Hartsel, the nucleus of his future ranching empire. His herd consisted of longhorn cattle imported from Texas.

To diversify his herd, in 1864 Hartsel went to Missouri to bring back one hundred Durham red shorthorns (shorthorn and red Angus mix) and one white shorthorn bull. The drive was planned to last one year, but due to Indian uprisings on the Great Plains (precursor to the American Indian Wars of 1866–1890), the drive took two years, and two of his men were killed in Indian attacks. The first year, he got as far as Kansas, and in the summer of 1866, the cattle were finally at home on the Hartsel Ranch.

The 1925 *Country Gentleman* story said the Shorthorn Association credits solely Hartsel with introducing improved beef cattle to the "Far West," beginning when he drove the Durham reds from Missouri in 1865. It also says that even as late as 1925, "one notices among the mixed-breed cattle of South Park a tendency toward a white coat. It is the blood of [the] dead and gone white bull, a dominant strain which has prevailed."

Throughout the years living on the ranch, Hartsel had good relationships with members of the Ute tribe but had problems with the more hostile tribes—Arapaho, Cheyenne and Sioux. In 1868, a group of Arapaho (some historians say they were Cheyenne) took Hartsel captive. The aggressors had lost their way when pursuing their enemies, the Utes. Hartsel was released after he showed them the way out of the park.

More Than Cattle

Hartsel was one of the top cattle ranchers of his day, but that wasn't his entire business. He developed the hot springs at Hartsel for travelers. He also pumped the spring water to his home two miles away through a series of nine-inch-diameter hollow wooden logs.

The water wheel that pumped spring water to Hartsel's home. *Park County Local History Archives, South Park Historical Foundation.*

Throughout the 1880s, Hartsel added more diversity to the ranching operation. In 1882, more ranchers in South Park were growing barley, oats and potatoes to supplement livestock diets. At the Hartsel Ranch, there were twenty acres devoted to winter rye, winter wheat, barley and oats. The crops were doing "remarkably well," according to July 6 and August 10 editions of *The Flume.*

Hartsel was a cattleman through and through, and in 1885, he put a stop to his dispute with neighboring sheep rancher, F.P. Euler, by buying his land.

Ironically, three years later, Hartsel's view of raising sheep was reversed. *The Flume* reported on August 16, 1888, that Hartsel had added a flock of one hundred Southdown-Shropshire-mix sheep to his ranching operation. Hartsel sold the wethers (castrated males) and spring lambs from the flock and also sold wool.

"Whatever comes from these sheep is clear profit, since they take care of themselves, furnish summer meat for the family, hunt for their own food and, like chickens, come home at night to roost," he said in *The Flume* story.

And it was only a year earlier, in October 1887, when *The Flume* reported Hartsel was raising pork. He fattened the pigs on native grass, rye grass and milk from his dairy.

Hartsel sold beef, mutton and pork to mine owners to feed to their workers and shipped carloads of meat to city markets on the Colorado Midland Railway.

POLITICS

It would seem Hartsel had his hands full running the ranch and caring for his family, but he served the state as a member of the Public Land Committee of the Colorado Cattle & Horse Grower's Association and, in Park County, served as county commissioner and assessor.

MARRIAGE, FAMILY

On April 1, 1877, Hartsel married Nancy Boone Mayol. He was forty-two years old; his bride was thirty-one. She was a widow with two daughters, Amelia and Rose.

Sam and Nancy Hartsel had four children: a son, Samuel Bancroft Hartsel, who died in 1888 at the age of thirteen months; daughter Katharine, born in 1878; daughter Myrtle, born in 1882; and daughter Henrietta, born in 1886.

Hartsel Cemetery, deserted and neglected in July 2008. *Photo courtesy of David Stearns.*

Hartsel had a brother named Joseph Hartsel, who ranched at the head of Current Creek near Freshwater, Colorado, now called Guffey. Joseph Hartsel disappeared in 1901, and it was suspected that he was murdered. A reward of $1,000 was offered by Sam Hartsel and the county commissioners for an arrest of the "party causing his disappearance," said the August 28, 1903 *Flume* in a recap of events leading up to the discovery of Joe Hartsel's body.

The brother's disappearance was a mystery until August 1903, when a prospector by the name of W.T. Baker found Joe Hartsel's remains and the remains of a horse near a tree on the Joe Hartsel Ranch. It was determined that the two were killed by lightning, as evidenced by a torn boot and lightning damage to the tree, the August 28, 1903 *Flume* reported.

A service and burial were held in Hartsel on September 5, 1903.

Denver Move

The Hartsel's sold all but 240 acres around the hot springs of their Hartsel property in the fall of 1907 and moved the following spring to a house south of City Park on St. Paul Street in Denver. Nancy Hartsel, age sixty-four, died two years later in March 1910 of the grippe (influenza). She was buried at Fairmount Cemetery.

On August 22, 1910, the remains of family members Joseph Hartsel and Samuel Bancroft Hartsel (infant son of Samuel and Nancy Hartsel) were moved from the Hartsel Cemetery to a site near Nancy Hartsel's grave at Fairmount. The remains of Catharine Hartmann Hartsel, Samuel Hartsel's mother, were moved from a Cañon City cemetery on September 26, 1910, to Fairmount to be near the graves of the other family members. She died at the Hartsel Ranch in 1873.

Sam Hartsel was two days short of his eighty-fourth birthday when he died on November 20, 1918, nine days after World War I ended.

He did not have any illnesses and even, on the day of his death, had visited his offices in the then Ferguson Building at Seventeenth and Stout Streets in downtown Denver. Always busy, he spent his last years "investing and reinvesting his fortune in eight-percent real estate mortgages," said his longtime friend Frazer Arnold, who wrote the May 1942 *Colorado Magazine* article.

Hartsel is buried at the Fairmount Cemetery near his wife and family members.

Chapter 3

Tabor, Dyer, Howbert

Early County Settlers Crossed Paths Through
South Park on Journeys to Fame

S outh Park is a crossroads, as evidenced by strings of cars seen on U.S. 285, U.S. 24 and Colorado Highway 9, especially on holiday weekends in summer and fresh-powder ski weekends in winter. Some come to the park to stay; others are here for a short time, passing through on their way to distant destinations.

In the 1860s, members of three families who were prominent in Colorado history crossed paths in South Park on their journeys to fame. They were Horace and Augusta Tabor, who later made a fortune in Leadville silver mines in the 1870s; Father John Dyer, the Methodist "snow-shoe itinerant" preacher whose circuit covered South Park; and Irving Howbert, a man prominent in early Colorado Springs history who, in the summer of 1860, lived in Hamilton with his Methodist-minister father. He was a fourteen-year-old boy, and in his autobiography he included memories of life in the early mining camp.

THE TABORS

Background

Horace and Augusta Tabor traveled through South Park in the spring of 1860 on their way to Oro City and California Gulch, near Leadville.

Buckskin Gulch, 1864. *Park County Local History Archives, South Park Historical Foundation.*

They had come from a dry land farm in Kansas and were originally from Augusta, Maine.

They traveled via Colorado City (now part of Colorado Springs) to Leadville, partially over the route of today's U.S. 24. On that journey, Augusta Tabor recorded in her journal a first impression of South Park as seen from today's Wilkerson Pass: "I shall never forget my first vision of the Park. I can only describe it by saying it was one of Colorado's sunsets. Those who have seen them know how glorious they are."

After a little over a year in the Leadville area, as placer mining there declined, the couple came back over the Mosquito Range and lived in Buckskin Joe from 1861 to 1868. The town near Alma was sometimes called Laurette and wasn't officially Buckskin Joe until February 1866.

The Tabors are better known for their life after leaving Buckskin Joe.

In 1868, they went back to being storekeepers in Leadville, and in April 1878, Horace Tabor grubstaked two miners. (Grubstaking is the practice of advancing money to miners for food and supplies for a share in any profits.) In May, the two miners discovered the Little Pittsburg claim, one of Leadville's richest; the Tabors retained a one-third interest in the mine and became wealthy.

But the marriage was already failing. In 1880, when Horace Tabor met Elizabeth McCourt Doe, known as Baby Doe, Augusta and he were no longer together. When Horace and Augusta Tabor divorced after twenty-six years of marriage in January 1883, it was strongly contested by Augusta. Reported in the October 31, 1883 *Denver Republican* newspaper, the reason Augusta contested was not that she hoped to have Horace back, but so that no other woman could carry his name, she said.

But despite that history, when Horace Tabor married Doe two months later, it sent a whirlwind of malicious gossip through high society in Colorado and Washington, D.C., where Horace Tabor was three days short of completing a thirty-day senate term. He was appointed to the term after Senator Henry Teller resigned to serve as secretary of the Interior.

For ten years, Horace Tabor and his second wife lived lives of wealth and fame, and he had a somewhat successful political career, his highest office being two terms as Colorado's lieutenant governor. The two were financially ruined in the 1893 silver crash.

Augusta Tabor continued to prosper in her later years and, on her death in early 1895, was one of Denver's wealthiest citizens.

In Buckskin

But before all that fame, Horace and Augusta Tabor lived in Buckskin Joe. The couple had accumulated a small fortune already; Augusta estimated their wealth in 1861 at $7,000—in 2013 that's $184,000—earned through Horace's gold panning in the summer of 1860 and through a store the couple ran the following spring in Oro City. In June 1861, when both were about thirty years of age, the couple decided to chance a move to the new bonanza area, Buckskin Gulch.

When they arrived at their new home, the town had a theater, and for a while in 1862, it had a newspaper, the *Western Mountaineer*. Buckskin Joe had a reputation as a wild town, but visits from Father John Dyer helped balance that image.

Horace Tabor had less luck in the gold fields at Buckskin Joe, but the couple did well financially. He was the postmaster from June 1863 to June 1868, serving nearly to the end of the camp's existence. They had a general store and the post office in the front room of their home. Historians note that it was Augusta Tabor who most frequently ran the store and post office. She also took in boarders and laundry to supplement the family income.

When Horace Tabor wasn't placer mining, he took his turn minding the store. He was generous (with Augusta's hard-earned money) to customers who couldn't pay their bill, often grubstaking them.

He was the superintendent of schools in Park County for a time, and it was in Buckskin Joe that he developed an interest in politics.

DYER

Father John Dyer was a traveling Methodist minister who reached Buckskin Joe in July 1861, two months after he began a seven-hundred-mile journey on foot from Lenore, Minnesota. The date was within a month of the Tabors' arrival. He preached in South Park and surrounding areas until 1870, when he was transferred to the "Divide circuit," covering locations south and east of Denver in Douglas County.

His first impression of South Park, coming over Kenosha Hill, is recorded is his autobiography, *Snow-Shoe Itinerant*.

"From this point is a view of grandeur never to be forgotten," he said.

Dyer's book says that only three other preachers had ever been to South Park before 1861. One of those was William Howbert, father of fourteen-year-old Irving.

Carrying mail and traveling the passes of the Mosquito Range on foot and on snowshoes was not always an easy commute. In his autobiography, Dyer tells of one trip from California Gulch near Leadville to his home in Mosquito Gulch. It was a harrowing tale of snow slides, frozen feet and near death. When Dyer finally made it home and with a friend's help spent three weeks recuperating, he sent to "H.A.W. Tabor, our storekeeper, and paid him sixteen-cents-a-pound for corn to make hominy, which [Dyer] considered a luxury."

Dyer had a small cabin in Mosquito Gulch, and although he and the Tabors lived in the same general vicinity, they lived quite different lives. Throughout his book, Dyer talks about money, specifically how little he made and how much he could save. One February, Dyer had a meeting in Denver. There was a weekly stage from Buckskin with fare of ten dollars each way, but Dyer chose to walk the hundred miles. It took him two and a half days one way, but he saved twenty dollars on the round trip.

The Tabors, on the other hand, were well off when they arrived in Buckskin Gulch, and thanks to Augusta Tabor's work ethic, they remained in the upper class of mining-camp society.

HOWBERT

From August to December 1864, Irving Howbert, at age eighteen, was a corporal in the Third Colorado Calvary and, under its commander—Colonel John Chivington—was a participant in the infamous Sand Creek Massacre. It occurred in November 1864 when a Colorado Territory militia attacked and destroyed a village of friendly Cheyenne and Arapaho Indians in a massacre that included women and children, according to generally accepted historical records.

Howbert's autobiography, *Memories of a Lifetime in the Pikes Peak Region*, includes an eyewitness account of the battle that disagrees with historical records. He said that women and children were not attacked, although a few women that did not leave camp when the fight started were killed. The battle involved warriors of the Arapaho and Cheyenne tribes, he said, and "the number of warriors in the village was about equal to our force." He said the Colorado Cavalry attacked the Arapaho and Cheyenne in retaliation for attacks on wagon trains and settlements in Colorado and the torture and killings of its citizens in the three years before the Sand Creek battle. Evidence of attacks on settlers was found in the camp following the battle, including "more than a dozen scalps of white people, some of them from the heads of women and children."

What Howbert called an inaccurate account of the battle was made to Congress, he said, primarily by Lieutenant Colonel Samuel F. Tappan, an army rival of Chivington who gave an altered description of the battle to blacken Chivington's reputation. Howbert gave the reason that in 1862, Chivington was promoted over the envious Tappan.

By 1869, Howbert was elected El Paso County clerk and recorder, and in his career, he became one of the most influential men in the history of Colorado Springs. He became wealthy in Leadville silver mines, railroading and banking. The former town of Howbert, now buried under the waters of Eleven Mile Reservoir in southeastern Park County, was named for Irving Howbert, although he never lived in the vicinity.

But in the summer of 1860, Howbert was a fourteen-year-old boy who traveled west with his father, William Howbert, in search of riches in the Colorado gold rush.

Irving Howbert and his father met Chivington in 1860 when they first arrived in Denver. He was a presiding elder of the Methodist Church and was looking for someone to establish missions in the South Park mining camps.

Hamilton, 1867. *Park County Local History Archives, George D. Wakely photo, Ed and Nancy Bathke Collection.*

William Howbert was recruited and gave up the search for gold. He had previous experience as a Methodist minister in Iowa. According to Dyer's book, Chivington had joined the army by September 1861, and so he was not the presiding elder when Dyer was on the Methodist circuit.

Irving Howbert was as impressed as Augusta Tabor and Dyer were with his first view of South Park.

"My first view of the Park was from the top of [Kenosha Hill], and, young as I was, it made a lasting impression on my mind," he said in his autobiography. He described a beautiful valley and wooded hills framed by rugged mountains. "It was a scene I never have forgotten."

Young Irving saw the beginnings of Hamilton and Tarryall, rival mining camps across Tarryall Creek about two miles north of Como. Neither exists today, but at the time of the Howberts' arrival, five thousand lived in the area. Large numbers of gold seekers arrived every day, and large numbers left in disappointment, he said.

Some claims were paying out $100 to $500 per day per man, Howbert said. The claim young Howbert was hired to work while his father was on the preaching circuit was not so prolific; it paid $6 for three days' work of three men and a boy.

Within a day or two of the Howberts' arrival in Hamilton, Irving's father established a Methodist mission, and within a month or so a church was erected. It would have been built of rough-hewn logs and probably had a dirt floor, similar to the other buildings in town. There were no sidewalks, and Howbert said that it wasn't uncommon for a man on horseback to ride up to a store window and place his order without ever dismounting.

He said there were many saloons but very few stores because anyone coming to the mining camps of 1860s Colorado typically brought enough provisions to last six months.

Howbert said trout were plentiful in all the streams that weren't being placer mined. One had only to dip in a net to catch all the fish one wanted—a "not very exciting sport," he said in his book. He also said that "moderately good beef was obtainable, and deer and antelope meat was abundant."

Gold dust was the medium of exchange; everyone carried a buckskin bag with gold dust that was used to make purchases. Gold dust was rated on its purity; not all dust from the various camps was equal, but the gold from Tarryall Gulch was "about the purest in any in the Pikes Peak region," said Howbert.

The Howberts left Tarryall Gulch in the late summer of 1860 and settled near Colorado Springs.

Chapter 4

EARLY DAYS AT THE ORPHAN BOY

Fire in December 2011 Not Only Fire at Mine; Gold Production
Worth $486 Million in 2013 Dollars

A fire of unknown origin occurred on December 23, 2011, at the historic Orphan Boy Mine in Mosquito Gulch, according to the January 6, 2012 *Flume*, and that prompted a look back at the mine's rich history.

A twenty-foot-tall ore house, one of three structures that had survived the passing years, was destroyed in the December 23 fire. The structures remaining at the site after the five were a collapsed tool shed and the mine portal.

Orphan Boy Mine Orehouse, 1985. *Photo courtesy of Larry Frank.*

But that was not the only fire that has been reported at the Orphan Boy. In October 1907, a bunkhouse burned to the ground. Miners were asleep when it started.

"The bunkhouses on the Orphan Boy mine burned down last week. Miners asleep in the building had to hurry up to get out in their nightdresses. Most of them lost their clothing and bedding, and several valuable watches were also among the lost articles," said the November 7, 1907 *Flume*.

Gold Value

About $7 million in gold was taken from the Orphan Boy over the years it was in operation, a time when gold never exceeded $20 per ounce, said William Jeffries in a report written in 1990 and stored at the Park County Local History Archives. His great-uncle was James Moynahan, owner and later manager of the Orphan Boy.

Assuming the weight of 350,000 ounces and knowing that the value of gold per ounce as of May 28, 2013, was $1,388.80, the gold taken out of the Orphan Boy would be worth about $486 million in 2013. That figure does not include the value of other minerals taken from the Orphan Boy in its 109-year production history.

Buildings

In August 1903, a *Flume* legal notice said there were several buildings at the Orphan Boy site, including "an engine house with a boiler, air compressor, and other fixtures therein, a blacksmith shop, a boarding house, a bunk house, an assay office, ore buildings, railroad track, and air pipes and other fixtures."

The legal notice advertised a sheriff's sale of the Orphan Boy, including twenty-four other lodes and mining claims, known collectively as the Orphan Boy Hill Consolidated Mining Co.

"It seems that the mine ran out of 'good' ore around the turn of the century and [the mine] was sold in order to satisfy the debts of the company," said an e-mail from Larry Frank, mining historian, former curator of Colorado Springs–based Western Museum of Mining and former director of Leadville's Healy House Museum.

Sheriff Silas D. Pollock forced the sale on August 31, 1903. The property was sold for $21,024.94 plus $7.95 in costs and was bought by S. Everett Hunter of the Kennebec Mining Co.

The ore house that burned in 2011 was likely part of the 1903 sheriff's sale.

"The ore house was built in the late 1880s or early 1890s by the Orphan Boy Hill Consolidated Mining Co. on leased land, where they began driving a crosscut tunnel to access the ore from the Orphan Boy, Senate, Honeycomb, New Years, Evening Star, Copper and Good Samaritan veins," said Frank in the e-mail. "This tunnel cut all of the major veins that had been mined in the early years." The cut went down low on Loveland Mountain adjacent to the railroad, he said.

BEGINNINGS

The Orphan Boy was considered old as early as August 1879; *The Flume* even then called it "the old Orphan Boy mine."

It was discovered in 1861, as reported in "Park City and Mosquito," an article in the August 26, 1880 *Flume* telling of the area's brief twenty-year history. It was one of the first Alma-area gold discoveries.

The mine was staked in 1862, and "it received the first patent number in the Leadville Land District, No. 37. Numbers 1–36 were reserved for the section number in a township," said Frank. The patent date was January 19, 1870.

In the spring of 1862, the town of Sterling had been established to support the growing number of mines in Mosquito Gulch, including the Orphan Boy. By the summer of 1862, there were four stamp mills, thirty houses, three saloons, two stores and more than one blacksmith shop at Sterling.

In just a few short years, $3.5 million in gold was taken from the Orphan Boy alone, *The Flume* reported in the August 26, 1880 edition. The camp was booming.

But the boom was short lived. In about 1865, the easily worked quartz-based gold began to play out; miners had to dig deeper, the gold was harder to get to and there was less gold to the ton. The deeper they dug, the more galena they found. Galena is the natural form of lead and often contains significant amounts of silver. In later years, silver, copper and zinc were mined from the Orphan Boy, but in 1865, the appearance of galena "was considered a loss to the miner," as reported in *The Flume*'s "Park City and Mosquito" article.

In 1866, the Indian Wars started, and because supplies were hauled across the Great Plains, freight charges increased considerably. The government recruited men to fight the war, others went "back to the states" (see *Flume*, August 26, 1880) and, of the remaining miners, most went to new gold fields in Montana. The mines caved in and filled up, and in the years before 1879, the name of Sterling was forgotten. There were only a dozen miners left working claims in Mosquito Gulch.

SILVER MINING, MOSQUITO AND PARK CITY

The Leadville silver boom started about 1878, and the Mosquito Pass toll road was built during 1878 and 1879 to give a direct route to Leadville. Its completion in July 1879 brought in some settlers, who took up claims in Mosquito Gulch. "The miners found plenty of indications of silver in the vicinity of the old mines," said the August 26, 1880 *Flume*.

The deserted site of Sterling was christened Mosquito, and the town site was reestablished. Some settlers moved into the old homes; others built new. In 1879, new businesses in the town of Mosquito included a store, a restaurant, a hotel and a blacksmith shop.

Mosquito wasn't the only town in the gulch; Park City was another new settlement.

In 1879, Henry J. Bagley, formerly of Denver, built a store east of Mosquito that carried a full line of goods to supply the mining camp. And he built a house for himself; his wife, Marg; and their two children, Henry, ten, and Joseph, three.

Michael Pyne built a hotel, and the structures together "formed the nucleus around which is built the town of Park [City]," according to *The Flume*'s August 26, 1880 edition.

There were 106 people counted in the 1880 census living in Park City and Mosquito Gulch combined. Within a short time, the town boasted three hotels, a market, a mining exchange office and twenty-five homes. Bagley also ran the post office, carried the mail back and forth to Alma and was coowner with Frank Howe of the land on which Park City was built.

In *The Flume* of April 28, 1881, it was reported the Orphan Boy and War Eagle (later named Senator) lodes had produced $500,000 in silver in four years of mining. A specimen assay that year showed 250 ounces of gold and 3,000 ounces of silver per ton.

Mosquito Gulch, 1880s. *Park County Local History Archives, T.C. Miller photo, Ed and Nancy Bathke Collection.*

LONG-WORKED MINE

The Orphan Boy was worked, off and on, beginning in 1861.

Through the years, the mine had problems and had to shut down occasionally for reasons such as water in the tunnels, litigation and management changes.

"The last that the mine was worked was when the mine dump was being reworked for the remaining gold values. I believe that was in the 1970s," said Frank.

ORPHAN BOY OWNER

The story of the Orphan Boy would not be complete without a short biography of its owner and manager, James Moynahan. He owned the Orphan Boy until the sheriff's sale in August 1903. He continued to manage the property after that sale.

According to the *Portrait and Biographical Record of Denver and Vicinity Colorado* of 1898, Moynahan was a Civil War veteran with the Twenty-seventh Michigan Infantry, fought at Vicksburg and Knoxville under General Ambrose Burnside and mustered out of the war as a captain.

In Park County politics, he served as county commissioner from 1870 to 1873. In 1876 and again in 1882, he was elected to the state senate,

James Moynahan. *Park County Local History Archives, Everett Van Epp photo, South Park Historical Foundation.*

representing Park and Fremont Counties. For two years, he was president pro tem of the senate, meaning he would act as governor if both the governor and lieutenant governor were out of state or unable to serve.

He was elected mayor of Alma in 1896, 1897 and 1898. He helped incorporate the town of Alma, was a member of the first board of trustees and assisted in laying out the town grid.

He was married to Mary Monaghan. They had four children: Alice, Ambrose Edwin, James W. and Clarissa.

Chapter 5

REYNOLDS GANG

Terrorizes County in July 1864, Buried Treasure Hidden and Unclaimed for Over 148 Years

A ccording to some historians, a treasure of stolen greenbacks and gold was buried in July 1864 in Park County near the head of Deer Creek, possibly in the Mount Evans Wilderness north of Grant, by a band of outlaws known as the Reynolds Gang. The estimated value of the buried treasure in 1864 was $63,000. On his deathbed in 1871, John Reynolds, the last living member of the gang, gave fellow outlaw Alfred Brown directions to the cache.

Stagecoaches such as this were targeted by the Reynolds Gang. *Park County Local History Archives, Alice McLaughlin Wonder.*

The money has never been found.

Parades in Park County today feature the "Reynolds Gang" walking down the street shooting black-powder weapons and followed by "the law," reenacting the shooting of the gang members and leaving them playing dead in the street.

The facts are hard to separate from rumors and story variations, but as near as can be determined, this is their story.

BACKGROUND

Jim Reynolds, leader of the gang of Confederate sympathizers, was born in Texas in the 1840s. In December 1859, he arrived in South Park with his brothers John and George and Aaron Briggs, a brother-in-law. Together with a group of brothers named Reed, the Reynolds group owned the Discovery placer claim along the South Platte River in Fairplay.

By November 1861, when Park County was named one of the first seventeen Colorado counties, Reynolds and his brother John, along with Jake Stowe and thirty-seven others, were imprisoned at Camp Weld for aligning with the Confederacy.

Camp Weld was located at what is now the corner of Eighth Avenue and Vallejo Street southwest of downtown Denver. Union troops based at this camp were Colorado Civil War volunteers who fought against the South in the Battle of Glorieta Pass, New Mexico, and against the Plains Indians. A small monument sits in this now-industrial section of Denver in the corner of a parking lot.

John and Jim Reynolds and Jake Stowe returned to Texas after being set free the following spring. They came up with a plan to raise money for the South by robbing from those getting rich in the gold fields of Colorado. Originally, fifty men were recruited, but by the time they returned to Park County, the gang was down to nine members.

BEGINNING OF THE END

Their crime spree included robbing homes, ranches, stagecoaches and boardinghouses in locations ranging from the Guiraud Ranch—now the

Buffalo Peaks Ranch near the former town site of Garo in central Park County—to Conifer in central Jefferson County. They claimed all the bounty for the Southern cause in the War Between the States, although it is unknown if any of the money made it back to Texas and the Confederacy.

The raid that was the beginning of the end for the Reynolds Gang occurred on July 26, 1864, when the gang robbed one of Dan McLaughlin's stagecoaches. McLaughlin ran a stage station at the site where the town of Como is today. The lone passenger that day was William McClellan, owner of all the stage lines in the area, who was robbed of his watch and money. Absalom "Ab" Williamson, the stagecoach driver, had fifteen cents on him that was taken by the gang. If the gang would have followed the unwritten "code of the West" and not robbed the driver, their destiny might have been different.

Also taken was $3,000 in gold and letters from miners sending "greenbacks" home. The term "greenback" originated when the first U.S. paper money was printed, in about 1863 or 1864, with green ink on the back of the bill.

CAPTURE

The robberies escalated in number and aggression throughout the next few weeks until a posse was sent after the robbers, forcing the gang to take refuge in Hall Valley, north of the Kenosha Pass summit.

"A company of miners and others from Summit County" were the first to find "the marauders in camp at the head of Deer Creek," according to an article titled "Tales of Early Days" in the *Steamboat Pilot*, from Steamboat Springs, Colorado, of September 29, 1915.

The posse surprised those in the outlaws' camp, and the outlaws jumped on their horses and scattered. But before the posse arrived, the two Reynolds brothers had hidden the money away from camp in an old prospect hole.

During the posse's surprise attack, gang member Owen Singleterry (or Singletary) was killed and then beheaded by the posse. The head was brought back to Fairplay (or Alma or Montgomery) as a trophy. It was preserved in alcohol and on display for many years.

Soon after the gang scattered, another member, Tom Holman (or Holliman), was captured "on the road leading from the mines to Cañon City," according to the *Pilot* article. (This was probably on the current Colorado Highway 9.) Holman was taken to the Fairplay jail, where he was

Hall Valley, circa 1870s. *Park County Local History Archives, Boot-Hall Family Collection.*

threatened with death and forced to tell authorities of the gang's rendezvous point, which was on the top of a mountain near Currant Creek Ranch (near Guffey). Five more of the gang members were captured near the rendezvous site the next day, including Jim Reynolds, John Bobbitt, John Andrews, Jack Robinson and Tom Knight. Jake Stowe and John Reynolds escaped, although Stowe was severely wounded and probably died from his injuries.

John Reynolds fled to Santa Fe, New Mexico. Some sources disagree on the number of gang members who were captured and who escaped, but not of the final outcome.

No Mercy

The six gang members were taken to Denver and turned over to the custody of U.S. Marshals. They were later transferred to military custody because of their known allegiance to the Confederacy. On August 23, they were tried and found guilty by the military court.

They were placed in the charge of Captain Theodore G. Cree of Company A, Third Colorado Calvary, and ordered transferred to Fort Lyons, near La Junta in southeastern Colorado. Cree was under the direct command of Colonel John Chivington, both of whom became infamous for the Sand

Creek Massacre later in 1864. The wagon driver was the same Williamson, now a sergeant in the Third Colorado Cavalry, who was robbed of fifteen cents during the McLaughlin stagecoach robbery in July and who had not forgiven nor forgotten the Reynolds Gang.

Before beginning the trip to Fort Lyons, the prisoners were warned not to make trouble or they would be shot. Near the old town site of Russellville, close to today's Franktown in Douglas County, Colorado, the wagon carrying the prisoners fell behind the mounted escorts. Cree said that the prisoners tried to escape and his men were forced to shoot them. It was reported that Williamson was the one who fired all the fatal shots. The prisoners were left where they fell on the prairie, handcuffed and shackled together. There is speculation that Cree was given orders before the group left Denver to shoot them along the way. The journey to Fort Lyons took nine days in 1864, but no food was packed for the prisoners.

JOHN REYNOLDS

Meanwhile, John Reynolds was by that time living in Taos, New Mexico, and, in 1871, was dying of gunshot wounds he received when stealing horses. On his deathbed, he gave Brown directions to the hidden money. The directions were later published in the 1897 autobiography of Colorado lawman and detective David J. Cook titled *Hands Up; Or, Thirty-Five Years of Detective Life in the Mountains and on the Plains, A Condensed Criminal History of the Far West*:

> *Jim and me buried the treasure the morning before the posse attack on Geneva Gulch. You go up above there a little ways and find where one of our horses mired down in a swamp. On up at the head of the gulch we turned to the right and followed the mountain around a little farther, and just above the head of Deer Creek, we found an old prospect hole at about timberline. There we placed $40,000 in greenbacks, wrapped in silk oil cloth, and three cans of gold dust. We filled the mouth of the hole up with stones, and ten steps below struck a butcher knife into a tree about four feet from the ground and broke the handle off and left it pointing toward the mouth of the hole.*

1870s

Chapter 6

COLONEL FRANK MAYER

Buffalo Hunter, Civil War Drummer Boy, Author;
Met Dancehall Entertainer Silverheels When
U.S. Marshal of Buckskin

Colonel Frank Mayer was about two months short of his 104th birthday when he died at the old Fairplay Hospital in February 1954. The old hospital at 550 Castello Avenue is now an apartment house.

Colonel Frank Mayer, at age one hundred in 1950. *Photo from* The Buffalo Harvest; *courtesy of Pioneer Press, Inc.*

During his last twelve years, Mayer lived in a five-room house on Lot 2, Block D, in the town of Fairplay. That home has been structurally restored, furnished with period furniture from the era of Mayer's lifetime and is now one of seven structures on its original site in Fairplay's restored 1880s mining town museum, South Park City.

Mayer lived a full life, and he had so many occupations that when he was asked in 1935, at the age of eighty-five, to name them, he replied, "Well, sir, I've never been a bartender or a ribbon clerk, but I've tried everything else at least once and had a mighty fine time."

(The circa-1935 definition of "ribbon clerk" is one who is a small-stakes gambler or one who is a clerk in a fabric store measuring and cutting lengths of ribbon.)

BUFFALO RUNNER

Mayer is best known for the six years (1872–78) he spent as a full-time buffalo hunter—or runner, as they preferred to be called. He made his first buffalo kill, of an aging bull, in 1872 in Oklahoma and his last kill, another aged bull, on an elk-hunting expedition in Wyoming in 1881.

In the 1870s, Mayer saw the population of buffalo—which he acknowledged are more accurately called "bison"—decline rapidly as at least 10,000, and possibly as many as 20,000, men were involved in the "buffalo-killing trade." There were estimates of 20 million buffalo in the western United States before the buffalo harvest began in earnest in 1870, according to an article, "The Rifles of Buffalo Days," he wrote for the September 1934 edition of the *American Rifleman* magazine.

The men involved were "veterans of the Civil War," said Mayer in his book *The Buffalo Harvest*, cowritten with Charles B. Roth and first published in 1958 after Mayer's death. He said they were "at loose ends, wanting adventure, feeling the discomfort of claustrophobia at being cooped up in houses and towns after adventure in war."

By his own admission, he and others in the trade were ultimately responsible for the near annihilation of the buffalo and, because of that slaughter, responsible for the loss of Native Americans' ability to live independently on the land.

And that annihilation and slaughter were with the full support and cooperation of the U.S. government in the form of unlimited free ammunition, said Mayer.

DUAL PURPOSE

There were two reasons the government encouraged the buffalo slaughter, said Mayer cautiously, almost reluctantly, in *The Buffalo Harvest*. For one, buffalo were in the way of western expansion. The animal couldn't be

Mayer home in 1958. *Photo courtesy of South Park City Museum.*

Mayer home in 2012. *Author photo.*

controlled or domesticated. "He couldn't be corralled behind wire fences. He was a misfit. So he had to go," Mayer said.

Mayer said a "high ranking officer in the plains service" once told him the second reason that the government gave away free ammunition to buffalo killers. The officer said, "Either the buffalo or the Indian must go. Only when the Indian becomes absolutely dependent on us for his every need, will we be able to handle him. He's too independent with the buffalo. But if we kill the buffalo, we will conquer the Indian. It seems a more humane thing to kill the buffalo than the Indian, so the buffalo must go."

Mayer did not disclose the name of the "high ranking officer."

Civil War

But long before he ever hunted buffalo, Mayer was a drummer boy with the Union army in the American Civil War, when at thirteen he lied about his age and was recruited into the 165th Artillery. He was possibly following in the footsteps of his father, who was a Union army artillery officer, according to a story in the July–August 1986 edition of *Rifle Magazine*.

In April 1865, two years after joining the army, Mayer witnessed the surrender of General Robert E. Lee at Appomattox Court House, Virginia, he said in a 1953 story in the *Denver Post*'s *Empire* magazine.

He said he witnessed the battles of Gainesville and Gettysburg and was with General Burnside in December 1862 when Burnside's troops crossed the Rappahannock River before the Battle of Fredericksburg, Virginia. In that battle, two Union and two Confederate generals were killed, and the Union army retreated in defeat.

In the Battle of Gainesville (Florida) on August 17, 1864, Union forces marched into the town square in a move to occupy the city. They suffered severe losses and were defeated.

The Battle of Gettysburg (Pennsylvania) on July 1–3, 1863, saw more casualties—as many as fifty-one thousand combined in Confederate and Union forces—than any other battle in the Civil War.

Confederate forces were defeated, and the battle "is considered the turning point of the Civil War," according to the Library of Congress website at www.loc.gov.

In November 1863, President Abraham Lincoln, in dedicating the Gettysburg National Cemetery, gave the now-famous Gettysburg Address.

Mayer ultimately served in the U.S. Army for thirty-five years. After the Civil War, he fought in the Indian Wars on the American frontier and in the 1898 Spanish-American War, rising to the rank of lieutenant colonel, according to the *Empire* magazine story.

Silverheels

But Mayer wasn't always involved in killing and warfare.

In the August 26, 1948 edition of the *Park County Republican and Fairplay Flume*, Mayer said that as a young man, he was appointed U.S. Marshal in the town of Buckskin Joe, a former mining town in Buckskin Gulch west of Alma.

And in his tenure there, he met the legendary dance hall entertainer Silverheels, he told the reporter.

He said that the stories about her being a beautiful blonde were false, and in fact, she was a "gorgeous brunette."

"She arrived one day on a stagecoach" and had a contract to dance in one of the halls in the town, he said.

In his lifetime, Mayer visited every country except Siberia and Tibet as a mining engineer, he told the *Empire* magazine reporter, so when he said he had "never seen a more beautiful interpretive dancer in the world," as he said about Silverheels, it seemed likely that she was quite a dancer.

He mentioned in *The Flume* story some of her dances that were his favorites: "The Birth of Love," "Coming of Spring" and "Opening of the Lotus."

"When she danced, she wore a mask, sometimes a blue one, sometimes a white one, but she never showed her face," he said.

"As for her name, she had three pairs of dancing slippers, black, white and red, but they all had silver heels.

"Her audiences were prospectors and trappers, and every last man of them was infatuated with her. When she finished her dance, they'd throw their pokes of gold (small leather pouches for carrying gold flakes) on the stage, and I've seen as many as 54 pokes there."

"When the terrible smallpox epidemic broke out in Buckskin Joe, Silverheels worked tirelessly nursing the victims. She used her money to bring doctors from Colorado Springs and Denver."

Mayer said that when the smallpox epidemic was over in Buckskin Joe, many people left town, including Silverheels. She was never seen again, and he said, "The best we could do was to name the mountain after her."

AFTER THE BUFFALO

Mayer was married for less than half of his life. He and Marjorie Monroe married in 1877. They were married for forty-four years, until her death in 1921. He outlived her by thirty-three years, but tears came to his eyes even at age 103 when talking about her. "I buried my heart with her," he told a reporter in 1953.

He was a published author of three books: *The Buffalo Harvest*; *The Song of the Wolf*, published in 1910; and *The Unmuzzled Ox*, published after 1910 but with an unknown exact date. He wrote several magazine articles, most of those about hunting or guns. He was also a poet.

The Unmuzzled Ox is out of print, but *Buffalo Harvest* had a second printing in 1995. And *The Song of the Wolf* was reprinted most recently in 2010.

Mayer was satisfied with the life he led. In 1953 at age 103, as he was being interviewed for *Empire*, he said, "I have lived a full life. I haven't a single regret."

Note: The story of Mayer's life was compiled through magazine and newspapers stories written during and after his lifetime, much of it with direct quotes from Mayer, and through Mayer's book The Buffalo Harvest. *No written record was found of Mayer in the Civil War. Buffalo runners were nomadic individuals and difficult to tally in U.S. census records, and in fact, Frank Mayer was not found in the U.S. census until 1900. The story of Silverheels is traditionally told as taking place in the early 1860s, when Mayer was in his early teens and, by his own account, a drummer boy in the Union army.*

Was Mayer a truly extraordinary man, a teller of tall tales or a little of both? It's more than fifty years past his death, and the answer may never be known.

Chapter 7

CIVIL WAR VETERANS

*Settled in Park County Following War; How They Lived,
Where They Died*

In November 1861, when Park County was established as one of the seventeen original counties in Colorado, the Civil War was raging back East and in the Midwest. Other battles were being fought in the Colorado Territory.

In cemeteries and on pioneer homesteads throughout the county, one can find the graves of men who served in the American Civil War (1861–1865). Those who came to Colorado after the war needed a fresh start in a place that took them away from the devastation of battlefields. Some found it in the wide-open prairies, the high mountain valleys and the fertile wetlands of Park County.

Some of the veterans who came here after the war began new lives as miners and ranchers. Others became political leaders or found solitude living alone in the hills. But for all, the lives they led contributed to the history of early Park County.

From veterans' graves decorated with a military headstone, one learns the unit in which the veteran served, and from that, one can discover information on the soldier's military career. Hints from census records and newspaper obituaries add a touch of humanity to a decades-old grave. Of the military headstones I found, all mark the graves of former Union soldiers.

The few Confederate graves found do not have military headstones. Only the single word "Confederate" in a newspaper obituary tells readers of that part of a pioneer's history.

What the men had in common was that they lived, died and were buried in Park County in the years after the war. Their lives here were as unique as their military service records, but one thing they shared was patriotism on Decoration Day celebrations (now called Memorial Day).

Then, veterans from both sides of the battle and from all over the county gathered together to talk about war memories "of Shiloh and Bull Run, some pleasant, but most of them sad," *The Flume* of June 2, 1905 reported. At that celebration, veterans and their wives feasted on food the soldiers ate in the war: "coffee and hard-tack, corn-bread and bacon, pork and beans."

In addition to the few mentioned below, veterans' graves can be found at public cemeteries at Alma, Fairplay, Shawnee, Guffey, Buffalo Springs, Lake George, the Horn Cemetery near Bailey and in the private Lamping Cemetery near the former Webster town site. Two graves were found outside formal cemeteries, the grave of John Badger on County Road 92 near Wilkerson Pass and the grave of Benjamin Ratcliff on his former homestead off Tarryall Road near Jefferson.

DANIEL M. CLARK

Daniel M. Clark served first in Company E and later in Company G of the Second Colorado Cavalry, leaving the service with a rank of corporal. His obituary in the June 30, 1892 *Flume* began with "one of the very oldest citizens of Park County and even Colorado passed away at Alma last night." Perhaps "oldest" citizen was an exaggeration; the article went on to say Clark was fifty-nine years and three months old.

Clark was born in about 1834. He was a miner who came to Buckskin during the 1859 gold rush. He enlisted in the Colorado Cavalry in 1861, where he would have had the double duty of guarding the Colorado Territory and its gold mines from Confederate invasion and protecting white settlements from Indian raids. After he was released from the cavalry, he lived in Fairplay with his wife, Clara, and their son. It was not until the last months of his life that he began collecting a pension for his war service. In his final years, the family lived a secluded life in Buckskin Gulch. Clark had been in feeble health for some time when he died on June 29, 1892. He is buried at the Buckskin Cemetery near Alma.

The original military marker at Clark's grave disappeared. A new marker was placed on the grave in the week of August 7, 2011, through the government's policy of replacing missing markers at no charge on veterans' graves.

Grave of Daniel M. Clark at the Buckskin Cemetery near Alma in 2011. *Author photo*.

DAVIS HALLOCK

Davis Sperry Hallock, born in February 1833 in New York, enlisted in Company C, Fifth Iowa Cavalry, on September 22, 1861, at the age of twenty-one. He was honorably discharged on October 19, 1864, in Nashville. Originally from Nebraska, he married Sarah Steinman in 1869, and they lived in Missouri. Probably four of their eight children were born in Missouri before the family moved to Como, where four more children were born and raised. He was a dairy rancher and day laborer.

In the February 15, 1883 *Flume*, mention was made of a fiftieth-birthday dinner party, "one long to be remembered," with ten to fifteen neighbors in attendance. Information from the 1900 federal census shows Hallock lived in Como with his wife and four sons—ages twenty-four, twenty, seventeen and ten—and a daughter, age fifteen. They also had a lodger in the home, a twenty-four-year-old day laborer.

Hallock died of Bright's disease, a term that was used for many kinds of kidney problems, on May 6, 1901, at the age of sixty-eight and was laid to rest in the Como Cemetery.

MILTON GIBBS

Milton Gibbs was born in June 1840 in Jefferson County, Pennsylvania. He served with the Union forces in Company F, 211th Pennsylvania Infantry. He married his wife, Mary, in 1861. In May 1864, Gibbs was injured in the series of battles called the Bermuda Hundred, named after the town of the same name near Richmond, Virginia. In those battles, the Union army under Major General Butler threatened Richmond but was stopped by the Confederate army under General Beauregard. Gibbs had pain from his wounds for the rest of his life.

Gibbs and his wife were living in Iowa in 1878 when their son Calvin was born. Of their seven children, he was the only child to live to adulthood. In 1880, the family moved to Buena Vista, and in 1884, they moved to Platte Canyon, living at various times on a ranch near Slaghts (east of Kenosha Pass), at Insmont (two and a half miles southeast of Bailey) and at Chase, near Shawnee.

His obituary, which appeared in the January 22, 1909 *Flume*, said Gibbs was "clever to a fault, was proud and cheerful." Gibbs suffered from rheumatism and was bedridden the last year of his life. He died at the age of sixty-nine on January 19, 1909. He is buried near Shawnee between Bill Tyler Gulch and Gibbs Gulch.

JAMES L. "DOC" LOCKRIDGE

James L. Lockridge was born in Virginia and served with his five brothers as a Confederate soldier from that state, according to his obituary in the September 2, 1910 *Flume*. The 1900 federal census shows a birthdate of December 1846, making him fifteen in 1861 when the Civil War started. There is some discrepancy with his birthdate in the obituary. It says Lockridge was sixty-seven when he died in 1910, indicating a birth year of 1843.

Lockridge was referred to as "Doc" or "Dr." in several issues of *The Flume*. His grave marker shows "Dock," but no indication of medical training was found. Lockridge came to Park County in about 1875 and was a miner. He had interest in the Crescent and the Good Samaritan mines near Alma. In 1904, he broke his leg so severely that he spent three months in the county hospital while the leg healed.

He died at the County Hospital on August 31, 1910, after a lingering illness brought on by a stroke. He is buried in the Buckskin Cemetery near Alma. His headstone is a simple mortuary marker showing only the name "Dock Lockridge."

ANSON ALLEN

Anson Alonzo Allen was born at Port Ontario, New York, on April 23, 1837. He married Charlotte Sheldon Farnum at Two Rivers, Wisconsin, in 1857. They had seven children at the time the 1880 federal census was taken. Allen was twenty-five when he enlisted in Company D, Twenty-seventh Wisconsin Volunteer Infantry, in 1862 while the family was still living in Two Rivers. He was discharged with the rank of corporal at Brownsville, Texas, in August 1865.

The family homesteaded near Puma City in 1870, and that was their residence at the time of Allen's death on May 1, 1911. His obituary in the

May 5, 1911 *Flume* said "the oldest pioneer left on Tarryall Creek died at his home near Puma City on Monday morning." Allen was seventy-six years old and died of complications from the grippe (influenza). His six living children were at his side when he died. He is buried in the Lake George Cemetery.

E.W. HERSHE

Captain Emanuel W. Hershe was born in Carlisle, Pennsylvania, in August 1838. He was twenty-three in October 1861, when he joined the

Grave of Emanuel W. Hershe at the Fairplay Cemetery in 2012. *Author photo.*

Eleventh Iowa Infantry, Company H, in Muscatine, Iowa, his home since age twelve.

Hershe was later assigned to the Eighth Louisiana Colored Infantry. It merged into the Forty-seventh U.S. Colored Infantry in March 1864. The unit was composed primarily of freed or escaped slaves from Louisiana's plantations and was commanded by white officers. Hershe was an officer. He was injured in battle on March 5, 1864, at Yazoo City, Mississippi, and applied for an invalid's pension in June 1866.

Hershe's obituary, the first story on the front page of the December 8, 1911 *Flume*, said that he grieved his entire life for his bride, the former Minnie Bishop. They married on January 4, 1871, in Muscatine, Iowa. She became ill and died on November 29, 1872, at the age of twenty-two. She was buried in Muscatine. He never remarried.

In Park County, he lived in a one-room shack in the Horseshoe District southwest of Fairplay for thirty-two years, from 1879 to 1911, and had success as a miner there with his business partner, Michael Fogerty.

In his obituary, Hershe was described as a "quaint character with an education that placed him far above the average man." He died at age seventy-three, on November 28, 1911, in his Horseshoe cabin, a day short of the thirty-ninth anniversary of Minnie Bishop's death. He is buried in the lot that he chose in the Fairplay Cemetery.

LENT HALL

Lent Hall was born in Walhalla, South Carolina, on May 29, 1848. His obituary in the February 7, 1913 *Flume* said, "He was a Confederate soldier going into the war when a mere boy." If Hall entered the service at the beginning of the war, he was thirteen years old.

At his death, Hall owned a ranch near Fairplay. He was a former county commissioner, a former county sheriff and also served as a water commissioner for Park County.

In 1907, he was part of the crew that stocked the South Platte River with sixty-one thousand fish. *The Flume* of August 23, 1907, in reference to the stocking of fish, said, "Let the good work go on, and South Park will be the best fishing resort in Park County within a few years."

In 1878, Lent Hall married Tempy Hill in Tennessee. Six children were born into the marriage. They lived in Alma when first married, and they later moved to Fairplay.

Grave of Lent Hall at the Fairplay Cemetery in 2013. *Author photo*.

Hall was described in his obituary as "a strong character, [with] a kind and jovial disposition that won him a host of friends wherever he went."

He died on February 2, 1913, at the age of sixty-four years, eight months and four days. He had been ill for five months before his death with no hope of recovery. He has a large headstone at the Fairplay Cemetery shared with his wife. There is no military information on the marker.

Chapter 8

SHELDON JACKSON'S FAIRPLAY CHURCH

One of More Than One Hundred in Western U.S.;
Jackson Arrested, Jailed in Alaska; Contributed to
Settlement of the West

The Sheldon Jackson Memorial Chapel in Fairplay, built in 1874, has shared the corner of Sixth and Hathaway Streets with the original Edith Teter School building ever since the school was built in 1881.

Today, the chapel appears dwarfed by the imposing new South Park school complex, but the church is holding its ground, much as its namesake—Sheldon Jackson, the Presbyterian minister—did when he was falsely arrested and jailed in Alaska in August 1885, seven months after being appointed the territory's commissioner of education.

Charges against Jackson were dismissed when then president Grover Cleveland ousted four corrupt lawmakers in the territory of Alaska; their altercation with Jackson was the last straw for the twenty-second president, then in the first year of his first term.

Jackson built churches in at least twenty-two towns in Colorado, including Greeley, Golden, Colorado Springs, Monument, Pueblo, Lake City, Ouray and Fairplay, and he ministered at many more sites where the population was too transient or the conditions too harsh to build a church.

The Colorado churches are included in the one-hundred-plus Presbyterian churches Jackson established in the western United States.

Sheldon Jackson, 1899. *Alaska State Library Photograph Collection, photograph by Frank La Roche, Seattle, Washington.*

PHYSICAL DISADVANTAGE

A native of New York, Jackson graduated from Union College in that state in 1855 and Princeton Theological Seminary (New Jersey) in 1858. He wanted to minister overseas, but the Presbyterian mission board told him it didn't think he was physically able to handle the hardships. He was about five feet tall with weak eyes and was reportedly often ill.

Because of that, the mission board kept him in the United States and its territories. His first job was as a teacher with the Choctaw tribe in Oklahoma. From there, he built schools, missions and churches in the vast area of the western United States, including Alaska, and proved that a small physical stature was not a disadvantage in his work.

Early photo of Sheldon Jackson Chapel in Fairplay. *Park County Local History Archives, Harold Sanborn postcard, Wilbur Lewis Collection.*

FAIRPLAY

Jackson arrived in South Park in 1872, when he "made the trip by stagecoach to the little gold-mining town of Fairplay," according to the 1945 article "Sheldon Jackson, Experience in Colorado in 1871" by Reverend J.N. Hillhouse, a Presbyterian pastor (1891–1960) who ministered in Fairplay. (The publication name was not on the clipping found at the Park County Local History Archives.)

In Fairplay, Jackson connected with a group of Christians, and together they organized the "First Presbyterian Church of Fairplay, Colorado Territory," according to Hillhouse. Two years later, the congregation was still active, and Jackson was instrumental in building the one-room Victorian Gothic church now called the Sheldon Jackson Memorial Chapel. It was dedicated at the Sunday service on October 4, 1874.

The chapel is still in use today by the South Park Community (Presbyterian) Church.

MOUNT BROSS

Jackson also visited the more remote areas of South Park.

For example, there was a "mining camp on Mount Bross," where two men were living with their families, according to the 1908 book *Sheldon Jackson: Pathfinder and Prospector of the Missionary Vanguard in the Rocky Mountains and Alaska*, by Robert Laird Stewart.

That book said the men were asked by a Dr. Field, who spent the summer of 1871 visiting churches in Colorado, if they "ever have preaching up here?"

The reply was "Oh, yes, Sheldon Jackson was up here last Sunday and we all met in this building [a house for crushing ore, the largest in the place]; and he stood upon the engine and gave us a rousing sermon."

Field was quoted in Stewart's book as saying, "That is the sort of men needed in these frontier settlements, men who can stand on an engine and preach."

He said that his friend Jackson is the sort who "would not hesitate, if he thought he could save an old hardened sinner, to mount a locomotive and let fly a Gospel message at a group by the wayside while going at a speed of forty miles an hour."

Jackson evidently was that kind of man. The Presbyterian mission board frequently found that by the time it had given him instruction to visit a new territory, Jackson had already been there and often had moved on, "leaving behind a string of new Presbyterian churches," said the 1977 National Register of Historic Places application for the chapel.

Denver

Before climbing to the peak of his career in Alaska, Reverend Doctor Jackson was based in Denver, arriving in February 1870, according to Stewart's book. He lived in Denver for eleven years.

He was ordained an evangelist following graduation from Princeton Theological Seminary and received an honorary doctor of divinity degree from Hanover College in Indiana in 1874 and honorary doctor of law degrees in 1897 from Union College in New York and Richmond College in Ohio.

Jackson was appointed superintendent of the Presbyterian Board of National Missions for Wyoming, Colorado, New Mexico, Arizona, Utah and Montana in 1869.

While in Denver, Jackson published the *Rocky Mountain Presbyterian*, a publication that varied from a weekly to a monthly newspaper and included woodcut pictures of places throughout the West in each issue. It was printed from 1872 to 1882. A partial collection containing original editions from its first seven years is archived at Hanover College in Hanover, Indiana.

"In 1871, he helped organize the [Presbyterian] Synod [or church council] of Colorado," said the Hillhouse article. The synod, still active today, is now called Synod of the Rocky Mountains.

Alaska

Jackson first went to Alaska in 1877, and that year was given the job of first ordained minister to Alaska. He was appointed the Alaska Commissioner of Education in 1885 and founded missions and, later, schools for the Native Alaskans. In about 1891, he began importing reindeer to Alaska from Siberia and Norway because there was not enough food in Alaska.

Sheldon Jackson Chapel in
Fairplay in 2012. *Author photo*.

IMPORTED REINDEER

The natural food sources for the Native Alaskans—whale, seal, moose, caribou, deer and sea otter—were being depleted due to "the remorseless devastation of the white man in his unceasing slaughter" of Alaskan game, according to a February 21, 1900 story in the *Colorado Transcript* of Golden, Colorado.

The Native Alaskans were starving; reindeer were well suited for the Alaskan environment and were useful for meat and milk. Their hides were used for shoes and clothes.

Reindeer are not native to Alaska and were not there until the animals were imported by Jackson, according to the University of Alaska–Fairbanks website. Reindeer are the smaller, domesticated cousin of the Alaskan native animal caribou.

Shipping the animals from Siberia was not easy, but shipping from Norway was a long, hard journey. A newspaper article dated February 5, 1898, in the *Rocky Mountain Sun* from Aspen, Colorado, said that the steamer *Manitoba* was en route from Norway with "530 reindeer and 87 Laplanders, men and women." The men and women were coming to Alaska to care for the reindeer. The ship also carried five hundred tons of Iceland moss to feed the animals. It took two weeks to fill the vessel and another two weeks to travel from Norway to New York.

The story didn't include information on how the group got from New York to Alaska.

ALASKA ARREST

Jackson took his ministry over one million miles in his lifetime, according to www.yukonpresbytery.com. From his hometown of Minaville, New York, he crossed the mainland United States and the territory of Alaska many times, establishing missions and schools, and he traveled to Siberia and Norway several times over the years in his work of importing reindeer to Alaska.

Since he was apparently a good man, one may wonder why he was arrested by the United States marshal of the Alaskan territory and why the arrest was approved by the governor and local district attorney.

Jackson was charged in May 1885 with "the crime of unlawfully, illegally, willfully and maliciously, and with malice, obstructing a certain road or highway," or so the warrant read. Specifically, the accusation was obstructing a public highway with a fence and buildings.

The fence and buildings were part of a school that Jackson had built. The new government officials, who took office in the fall of 1884, did not want Native Alaskans in school, and therefore, didn't want any schools built, according to Stewart's book. Those facts were echoed by Jackson in an 1886 pamphlet he wrote, "Statement of Facts Concerning the Difficulties at Sitka, Alaska in 1885."

Jackson wrote, "But, very strangely and unexpectedly, Governor Kinkead, United States Judge Ward McAllister, Jr., United States Marshal Hillyer, and Deputy Marshal Sullivan directly or indirectly threw their influence against the schools, and the native parents soon learned that the officers did not care whether they sent their children to school or not.

"The most open opposition, however, came from United States District Attorney E.W. Haskett."

A bench warrant was issued for Jackson, bond was set at $2,000 and a trial date was scheduled for November 1885.

According to the Stewart book, the officials behind the warrant were "zealously against" Jackson because he was building schools and educating the Native Alaskans. He was, in fact, at first charged with "working on school buildings" and "asking for a hearing before a Grand Jury." Those charges were dropped.

Jackson was compliant with the warrant conditions, continued his attention to building schools and teaching in Sitka and Juneau, Alaska, and would have appeared for trial in November 1885, but he didn't get that chance.

In August 1885, Jackson boarded a steamer with supplies to build a school in Wrangell, Alaska, southeast of Sitka. Before the ship left port, Jackson was arrested, "hustled off the steamer and locked in a (jail) cell," said Stewart in his book. The reason given for the arrest was that Jackson's bond had been increased to $3,200, and he needed to pay the increased amount.

Jackson paid the bond. He was released, but the steamer had left port by the time he was free to go. Steamers went south once a month, so the authorities had taken away a large part of the Alaskan construction season by delaying his journey for thirty days.

The arrest was witnessed by tourists and "lawyers and ruling elders" of the Presbyterian Church, which "aroused indignation" and President Grover Cleveland was contacted, according to the Stewart book.

An article in Explore North, www.explorenorth.com, an online site focusing on the "circumpolar North"—or lands surrounding the North Pole, including Alaska—talks about the political climate of 1884–85 in the Alaskan Territory.

It says, "Never before had so 'colorful' a group tried to govern a state or territory—alcoholism, fraud, just plain incompetence, and mental 'irregularities' were rampant at all levels of the new government."

The arrest and jailing of Jackson was the final mistake that forced Cleveland to replace all of the officers who were responsible for the charges brought against Jackson. A newly appointed district attorney dismissed the remaining charge.

DEATH

Jackson was planning to attend meetings of the Presbyterian general assembly on May 20, 1909, in Denver to reconnect with old friends and to visit some of the chapels he had built in Colorado in the 1870s, according to his obituary printed in the *Yuma Pioneer* from Yuma, Colorado, on May 14, 1909.

But on May 2 in Asheville, North Carolina, he died. He was sixteen days short of his seventy-fifth birthday. Jackson is buried in his hometown of Minaville, New York.

Chapter 9

FAIRPLAY'S FRONT STREET IN 1878

Following Fire in 1873, Business District Rebuilt

W alking along the boardwalk of Fairplay's Front Street today, one may get the feeling of stepping back in time. But if the clock could be turned back to the summer of 1878, there would be noticeable differences between then and now.

One thing that has changed is the variety of businesses. Fairplay was named the county seat in 1867, and it was in the midst of the gold- and silver-mining boom. As such, it was the area's supply and service center for miners, ranchers and settlers.

Along Front Street alone, stretching from about Sixth Street northwest to Second Street, were headquarters for two of the three Fairplay-based stage lines. There was a newspaper, a grocer, a brewery, two billiard halls, two hotels, a jeweler, a blacksmith and at least two saloons. There were stores selling dry goods and millinery (women's hats), jewelry, hardware and drugs.

The land office was here, and one could find the services of a doctor, attorney, banker, blacksmith and tailor on the main business street of Fairplay.

One would also notice that all of the structures were new. There were no buildings older than five years on the Front Street of 1878.

And that is because, even though Fairplay's beginnings were in the 1859 gold rush, the business district of the town's infancy was destroyed in a raging fire in 1873.

FIRE

At 8:00 p.m. on Friday, September 26, 1873, a fire started in the Fairplay House Hotel on Front Street. It is probable that the hotel was near Sixth and Front Streets, where its replacement was built after the fire.

Within five minutes of the fire's discovery, the second story of the hotel was aflame. It had been a dry summer, the town was built completely of wood and there was no water and no fire department to fight the fire.

Business houses were close together, making the fire spread quickly up the street. It was determined that to save the town, buildings would have to be blown up. But there wasn't enough explosive powder in Fairplay to accomplish that; the powder was stored at the mines.

The fire swept from Sixth Street, northwest up Front Street to the end of town, leaving the business district in ashes. The wind blew sparks into homes half a mile away and set them on fire. One witness said flames could be seen twenty-five miles away, according to a story in Georgetown's *Daily Colorado Miner* of September 28, 1873. Timing of the fire made the situation worse; two-thirds of the population had no shelter, and winter was coming.

The printing presses and equipment at Fairplay's newspaper, the *Sentinel*, were destroyed, but the story was covered in the *Daily Colorado Miner* and other Colorado newspapers, reprinted from a *Rocky Mountain News* story of September 29, 1873.

The good news was that there was no report of casualties, and all the legal papers from the land office and county clerk's office were saved.

FOUR YEARS LATER

A correspondent of Pueblo's *Colorado Weekly Chieftain* visited Fairplay and Alma twice during the winter of 1877 and early summer of 1878. The stories appeared in the November 8, 1877, and June 27, 1878 editions. Following are just a few of the people and places that the correspondent wrote about in the late 1870s; their stories give insight into Fairplay in its youth.

Newspapers

At the time of the fire, there was one newspaper in Fairplay, the *Sentinel*, owned by Dick Allen. In the *Daily Colorado Miner*'s introduction to the reprinted fire story, there were special "heartfelt sympathies" extended from the *Miner*'s editor to Allen, who came across the misfortune of the fire "just at a time when he had everything paid for, and his business was getting a fair start as a prosperous enterprise."

Allen rebuilt the *Sentinel* after the fire. In 1878, he was still the owner and employed W.S. Howell as editor. A rival newspaper, the *Mount Lincoln Times*, was published in Alma and was run by W.F. Hogan. It later moved to Fairplay.

The *Chieftain* correspondent, who signed columns with the name BONA (in all caps), indicated the two newspapermen didn't get along. He called Hogan "a genial cuss" who made "a live paper of the *News*." He said the paper had a good circulation throughout Park, Lake and Summit Counties and that Hogan "is happy."

But he said Hogan and Allen fought like "the Turks and Russians," (a probable reference to the Russo-Turkish War of 1877–78), and at the time of his visit, they were indulging in a pastime of "calling each other all the names they can conjure up from the Billingsgate dictionary." (Billingsgate was slang for foul, abusive language.)

Bank

The bank, established in 1872, was owned by Curtis G. Hathaway, who named the bank after himself, "Hathaway's Bank." In the 1873 fire, the bank building was destroyed, but Hathaway saved his money and papers. One of the first brick structures in town was the rebuilt Hathaway's Bank.

In 1887, the Independent Order of Odd Fellows lodge was established on the upper floor of the bank, where members still meet today. The main level of the building is also in use in 2013, occupied by the Fairplay Antique and Art Gallery.

Hathaway was a town trustee and agent for the Northwestern Stage Company, with service from Colorado Springs to Leadville. He had a branch bank in Alma (the Bank of Alma) and ran unsuccessfully in the race to become Colorado's lieutenant governor in the 1888 election. In 1897, he died of consumption in Tucson, Arizona. Both banks were taken over by J.H. Singleton in 1898; he was cashier at the Alma branch.

A.E. Jones Store and Hathaway's Bank, circa 1880s. *Park County Local History Archives, T.C. Miller photo, Ed and Nancy Bathke Collection.*

In 2013, the former A.E. Jones Store and Hathaway's Bank are now Miner's Moving & Storage and Fairplay Antique and Art Gallery. *Author photo.*

Billiard Halls

In 1878, there were at least two billiard halls on Front Street. One, the Eclipse, was run by the "big and fat and good natured" Fritz Coleman, said the November 8, 1877 *Chieftain* story. It was located "hard by the bank" (very close to the bank), said the June 27, 1878 edition.

A speculation is that this is today's yellow brick building with signage indicating occupancy by Miners Moving & Storage, although no definite source could be found. It is so close to the former Hathaway's Bank that the two look like one building. It is known that during its history, this structure housed at different times the store of A.E. Jones, the Senate saloon and the *Park County Republican and Fairplay Flume*.

Across the street from the Eclipse, according to the June 27, 1878 *Chieftain*, was the two-story Cabinet Billiard Hall owned by John J. Hoover. The billiard hall was upstairs, a liquor store was on the main level and a "sample room" was at the back of the billiard hall, "where the best of wines and liquors in the market are sampled by his thirsty customers," according to the November 8, 1877 *Chieftain*.

In April 1879, billiard hall owner Hoover shot and killed Thomas Bennett at the Fairplay House Hotel and was charged with first-degree murder. A year later, in April 1880, the court allowed Hoover to plead guilty to manslaughter. After receiving what some thought was too mild a sentence, a group of vigilantes broke Hoover out of the county jail and hanged him from a second-floor window of the Park County Courthouse. That structure, in 2013, houses the Fairplay Library.

But in June 1878, BONA said Hoover was "one of the best men in the business in the state," and the previous November, he said Hoover was "one of the best known businessmen of Fairplay."

Brewery, Saloon, Meat Market

Farther up the street was the South Park Brewery, also known as the Summer Brewery.

The June 27, 1878 *Chieftain* story said Leonhard Summer was one of the best brewers in the state, with a beer that "takes rank along with Zang's Denver and the Golden beer [a reference to Coors]." Zang's was a brewery and in 2013 is a brewpub restaurant in Denver.

Summer brewed South Park Lager Beer from his brewery located at about Third and Front Streets. The first brewery on the site burned in the

1873 fire; the structure mentioned in both of the *Chieftain* stories was built in 1875. The 1875 brewery building was destroyed by a fire in 1892. Summer rebuilt again, and that structure is the one currently seen at the South Park City Museum, a restored mining town in Fairplay.

Summer had a brother named Joseph Summer who was proprietor of Summer's Saloon, across Front Street from the brewery. BONA said Joseph Summer's saloon was "one of the popular resorts of the town. A pretty [young woman from Germany] sets them up at this place and the boys all go there when they are thirsty."

In 1879, Leonhard Summer built his own saloon on Front Street; the building is now part of the South Park City restored mining town. By 1897, Leonhard Summer had turned his saloon into a meat market, according to *The Flume* of December 10, 1897.

In July 1883, at the age of forty-three, Joseph Summer committed suicide at a Como saloon he had recently rented. It was believed that he suffered from temporary insanity, reported *The Flume* of July 13, 1883.

Leonhard Summer died by suicide on September 10, 1900, when he was sixty-two years old, apparently despondent over financial losses, *The Flume* of September 13, 1900, said. By the end of the month, the September 28, 1900 *Flume* reported that the meat market was leased to a Leadville man.

Hotels

The Fairplay House Hotel on Sixth Street had proprietor and ownership changes almost yearly, according to advertising in *The Flume* through the years. In 1877–78, the business was owned by Tom Kilduff. He was the brother of Alma's St. Nicholas Hotel owner, Ed Kilduff.

Brother Ed Kilduff stayed in the Alma area until at least 1909. But Tom Kilduff owned the Fairplay House for only a year and had left town by April 1879, when Hoover shot Bennett there.

When Tom Kilduff left Fairplay, he started a retail merchandising business in Kokomo in Summit County, Colorado. He later moved that business to Leadville, Colorado, and then to Aspen.

In 1885, Kilduff moved to Meeker, Colorado, and became a partner in a 3,500-acre cattle ranch. It was "one of the most imposing and profitable [ranches] on the Western slope" of Colorado, according to the 1905 edition of *Progressive Men of Western Colorado*, by A.W. Bowen & Co. publishers.

Another hotel mentioned by the *Chieftain* was near Second and Front Streets; the site is on the grounds of the South Park City museum. It was the Buckhorn Hotel, operated by G.J. (Jim) Cole.

He was formerly proprietor of an establishment called the Red Light Saloon in Pueblo, Colorado, and "he has here a number of the attractions which made the Red Light popular in Pueblo. Jim knows how to conduct a place of this kind and is a popular man in this vicinity."

The Buckhorn Hotel was also known as the Red Light Dance Hall. The girls who worked in this and other dance halls in the central Colorado Mountains were called "inmates" and not mentioned by name in newspaper stories of the day. Typically, the stories told of a dance hall–inmate's drug overdose or suicide. By 1883, the dance hall was closed and the building was being used to store hay. It burned to ashes at midnight on May 7, 1883.

1880s

Chapter 10

CRIME AND PUNISHMENT IN
1880s FAIRPLAY

People Protest Light Sentencing, Deliver Frontier Justice

Much like today, when crimes were committed in 1880s Fairplay, suspects were put in jail and defendants later had their days in court. Cases were tried by trained attorneys, and decisions of guilty or not guilty were determined by a jury of the defendant's peers. District and county judges passed judgment with a punishment deemed to fit the crime.

And also, much like today, some citizens disagreed with the verdict and made their opinions known. The difference is that today, one might write a letter to the editor or otherwise peaceably vent some feelings. In the 1880s, such venting could take a different, violent course of action.

IN THE 1880s

In Park County in the 1880s, the legal climate was, to put it mildly, quite different from today. In the days when shooting into the air on public streets was "getting to be a nuisance," according to *The Flume* of May 1, 1879, vigilante frontier justice was often taken to an extreme.

One example is the case of John Hoover. In April 1880, he was hanged by vigilantes from a second-story window above the double-door entrance to the Park County Courthouse. In 2013, the building is the Fairplay Library.

In 2013, patrons of the Fairplay Library enter the former courthouse below the window where John Hoover was hanged. *Author photo*.

Hoover was in jail awaiting transport to Cañon City. His sentence was eight years in the penitentiary for the unprovoked shooting of Thomas Bennett. The court accepted his plea of manslaughter.

HANGING AT THE COURTHOUSE

It was a few days past the full moon and very bright on April 28, 1880, when, shortly after 3:00 a.m., a small faction of the Fairplay population

This photo from 1880 shows the courthouse where John Hoover was jailed by the sheriff and later hanged by vigilantes. *Park County Local History Archives, T.C. Miller photo, Ed and Nancy Bathke Collection.*

took matters into their own hands. The masked and still-unknown vigilantes broke Hoover out of jail and hanged him from a second-floor courthouse window.

COURT PROCEEDINGS

In court the day before, Hoover was allowed to withdraw his first-degree murder plea of not guilty by reason of insanity and change the plea to guilty of manslaughter.

Hoover said in his deposition that he had mental problems that went back to an accident he had in 1871 in Oro City near Leadville, Colorado. He fell sixty-five feet down the Printer Boy mineshaft. The injuries caused "great and lasting injuries upon [his] head and spine," and they were such that they produced "unconsciousness and mental derangement of mind." Hoover said he never recovered and that the injuries caused "temporary fits of insanity."

Even with "mental derangement" and "fits of insanity," Hoover was able to build, own and manage the Cabinet Billiard Parlor at Fifth and Front Streets and serve on the Fairplay town board.

Only three witnesses could prove his statements, Hoover said in his deposition, and none was able to travel to Fairplay at the time court was in session. Hoover was advised by his lawyer to plead guilty to manslaughter.

District Attorney C.W. Burris accepted the plea, and Judge Thomas Bowen gave Hoover a sentence of eight years at the penitentiary. The sentence for manslaughter in 1880 was ten years. Hoover was allowed credit for the year he served in the county jail and another year of credit because he pleaded guilty, thus saving the cost and time of a trial.

The April 29, 1880 *Flume* reported that Hoover was "beaming with satisfaction" as he was led out of court.

HOOVER'S CRIME

On April 1, 1879, a year before the lynching, Hoover shot Thomas Bennett once in the chest with a double-action .38-caliber six-chambered Colt revolver, according to Sheriff John Ifinger's deposition taken two days after the shooting.

In 1879, John Hoover shot Thomas Bennett at the Fairplay House (aka the Fairplay Hotel), shown here circa the 1880s. *Park County Local History Archives, South Park Historical Foundation.*

It happened at 2:00 p.m. after Hoover stormed into the Fairplay House Hotel, near Sixth and Front Streets, and confronted Bennett as he was waiting at the counter.

LEADING UP TO MURDER

Bennett had been hired by the proprietor of the Fairplay House, J.H. McLain, "to clean out a ditch opposite the hotel." Hoover had complained previously about the ditch, saying it was a nuisance and that he would shut it off, which was why it was being cleaned, reported the April 3, 1879 *Flume*. The ditch supplied townspeople with fresh water and ran from Beaver Creek to the Middle Fork of the South Platte, according to an article in the October 2011 edition of the Park County Local History Archives newsletter.

The Fairplay House Hotel was on the south side of Front Street between Sixth and Seventh Streets. The ditch being opposite the hotel might have meant it was across Front Street on the north side.

The Hoovers lived in a home nearby, and the ditch "was running over and flooding the premises (home) of John J. Hoover," said *The Flume* of April 3, 1879.

Ironically, the Fairplay town board (and Hoover as a member) "ordered that the town ditch should be opened at once and kept open during the season," during a meeting reported in the March 6, 1879 *Flume*. The meeting was about a month before Bennett's murder.

IN COLD BLOOD

On April 1, 1879, Hoover left the Cabinet Billiard Parlor and "walked down the street and into the office of the (Fairplay House) Hotel," reported *The Flume* of April 3, 1879.

H. Dice (the first name was not recorded in court records) was one of three witnesses to the Bennett shooting and the one witness who interacted with Hoover that day. Dice said in a deposition on April 3, 1879, that Hoover walked up to the counter where Bennett was standing and said, "I own that house and lot, and I am going to run it, too. I am not going to have my family imposed on."

Dice said Bennett replied, "Hold on. I don't want any trouble and don't impose on anyone."

While Bennett was speaking, Hoover stepped back and fired, hitting Bennett in the chest. The bullet passed through his body and was found on the floor. Bennett was slumped over the counter when Hoover pointed his gun a second time, preparing for another shot. Dice stepped in front of Hoover and said, "For God's sake, don't shoot him again."

At that point, Hoover walked back out onto Front Street.

He was joined by his wife, Euphrasia Hoover, who had come out of their home near the hotel, and together they walked back to the billiard parlor. She advised Hoover to give himself up, and he did when the two met up with Sheriff Ifinger on the street near the billiard parlor, recorded the April 3, 1879 *Flume*.

When Bennett was asked if there was any reason for Hoover to shoot him, he said, "No, no, no, oh, my God, he did it in cold blood." The statement was made in a deposition taken at 4:30 p.m. on the day of the shooting

Bennett lived through the night and all the next day. He died at 7:30 p.m. on April 2, 1879.

THE HANGING

Not long before 3:00 a.m. on April 28, 1880, a crowd of men knocked on the door of Ifinger's home. They wanted the keys to the jail, which Ifinger would not give them. They searched the house and found the keys to the inner cells, said Ifinger in his deposition taken later the same day.

The mob also asked the guards at the jail for keys, but the guards told mob leaders they didn't have any. The mob broke down the doors to the jail and to Hoover's cell. The jail was in the basement of the courthouse at that time; the "new" jailhouse on the courthouse lawn was not built until November 1880.

The testimony of guard Walter Taylor explains the rest; picking up the story after the mob had taken the guards' guns and left the sheriff's office:

> *The next we heard they were on the stairs leading up to the courthouse.*
> *After this the crowd left in about 10 minutes, but just before they left they put our arms [guns] on the floor and we followed them out and found Hoover hanging from the front window.*

After the mob was away about 50 yards, we fired four shots to raise an alarm.
As they walked out they shook Hoover, and he appeared to be dead. Then
I proceeded after the Sheriff.

When he [Sheriff Ifinger] *arrived, I helped to take him* [Hoover]
down, and the rope offered as evidence is the one the hanging was done with
and I can identify it.

And the reason I did not cut him down I was satisfied he was dead and
thought I had no right to do so—I think there were about fifteen and I could
not identify any of them.

DETAILS

Hoover spent over a year in the Park County jail, from April 1, 1879, to April 28, 1880. *The Flume* of April 29, 1880, said the year of jail "had only slightly affected the rotundity [obesity]" of Hoover.

The vigilantes were never caught or identified. Sheriff Ifinger, in his deposition, said, "I am satisfied they had something in their mouths to deceive their voices and all being masked I could not tell who they were."

On May 6, 1880, *The Flume* reported that Judge Bowen and District Attorney Burris skipped town because they were scared that they would be hanged for their involvement in such a light sentence. The newspaper said, "Not one of the attorneys, the sheriff, or other officers of the law, except the district clerk, knew that court had adjourned." (Court adjournment refers to the judge closing a session of courtroom proceedings. In 1880, judges rode a circuit, visiting the many county seats to hold a court session about once every six months for about a week at a time, or however long it took to hear the cases that had piled up since the previous court session. Judge Bowen left Fairplay before the April 1880 session of court was over and before all the cases were heard, in effect not adjourning the court, except by telling the clerk that he would not be back.)

Bowen tendered his resignation as a judge at the end of May 1880 and later made a fortune in the gold fields of Rio Grande County and represented Colorado in the U.S. Senate.

Euphrasia Hoover was counted in the 1880 census on June 10. She was living in Fairplay with her brother, Ward Maxey; a sister, Helen Harlow (or Hellen, the spelling on her headstone at Fairplay Cemetery); and Harlow's eighteen-year-old son, James. The Harlows, from Maine, had been on an extended visit with Euphrasia Hoover since about the end of March 1880.

Harlow died of pneumonia on June 20, 1880, ten days after the census was taken. Her name is on the same monument that marks the graves of John Hoover and his daughter. Her obituary in the June 24, 1880 *Flume* indicates it was to be a temporary interment in Fairplay and that her husband would travel from Maine to Fairplay to bring her body home.

Euphrasia Hoover ran a millinery store in Fairplay at least since January 1880 (before the hanging). She sold the home on Front Street in November 1880 and in August 1881 became a manager of the same Fairplay House Hotel where her husband had shot Thomas Bennett almost two and a half years earlier.

In September 1883, Euphrasia Hoover married Chandler Potter, who was superintendent of the Moose Mine near Alma. The couple moved to San Pedro, Honduras, in December of the same year, where Potter "held a position of trust under the McLean Mining Company," as noted in *The Flume* of September 6, 1883.

Ward Maxey took over ownership of the Cabinet Billiard Parlor, renamed it Cabinet Parlor Billiard Hall and later became a successful sheep rancher.

John Hoover is buried in the Fairplay Cemetery near his infant daughter, Louisa, who died at eleven months old on December 29, 1878.

Chapter II

FORTY-SIX YEARS IN HOWBERT

*1887–1933: Former Ranching, Railroading Community
Covered by Eleven Mile Reservoir*

There's not much left of Howbert, Colorado, except fading memories and a few photographs.

The town and its two nearest neighboring communities—Idlewild and Freshwater Station—have been submerged since the late 1950s under the 117-foot depth and 3,405-acre expanse of Eleven Mile Reservoir at Eleven Mile State Park in southeastern Park County.

But before the abandoned towns were covered by the reservoir, they were the nucleus of a ranching community where people lived, worked, played and, eventually, died. After the railroad was established, Howbert was also a loading point for livestock and had a forty-two-car-capacity passing track.

Those facilities were used to ship the "largest cattle deal ever made in Park County," said the August 9, 1907 *Flume*. The Witcher ranching family sold eight thousand head in August 1907. "The cattle are to be gathered and shipped from Howbert on the Colorado Midland by December 1," it said.

BEGINNINGS

The Colorado Midland Railroad began operating from Colorado City (near the present-day intersection of U.S. 24 and Twenty-first Street in Colorado

Springs) to Leadville in 1887. As the track crossed South Park, the Midland established stations along the route, including Howbert at mile 52.1. It was named after the prominent Pikes Peak pioneer Irving Howbert.

The site was originally called Dell's Camp, probably for B.R. Dell, the proprietor of Dell's Store, which had been established at that site before the railroad came through.

The post office at Howbert was started in December 1887. A survey of the new town of 125 lots was completed in June 1888 and approved by the man who owned the property, James M. Petty. Streets were aptly named Dell, Midland and Petty.

BUSINESS

By September 1888, Dell was building a new store, "the largest building of its kind in the county," according to the September 27, 1888 *Flume*. He planned to use the upper floor for a church and meeting hall, the main floor for the store and the basement for storage. Construction was completed quickly. Less than a month later, the October 18, 1888 *Flume* reported the store was done, and Dell was moving his stock into the new location. The post office was also moved to Dell's new store.

The South Park Hotel in Howbert in 1894. It later became the Epperson home. *Park County Local History Archives, Harry C. Epperson Estate.*

Also in September 1888, Hardy Epperson was building the South Park Hotel and its adjoining shoemaker shop. He and his wife, Josephine, managed the Howbert Restaurant, likely inside the hotel. The Eppersons were residents of South Park as early as 1880.

A butcher shop was under construction, the Howbert Saloon sold "choice cigars and liquors" and a sawmill was turning out "lath in large quantities, as well as other lumber," according to 1888 issues of *The Flume*.

Howbert had a telegraph office, a drugstore, two more saloons, a depot, a schoolhouse, a blacksmith shop and "about 25 tar-papered houses," according to Harry C. Epperson in his 1944 book, *Colorado As I Saw It*.

The town also had a cemetery. It is believed to be on dry land, according to the Colorado Parks and Wildlife website, but its location is unknown.

LIFE IN HOWBERT

The Flume reported in the September 27, 1888 edition that "Howbert is the liveliest town in the county for its size."

And its size was small. The U.S. census of 1910 shows thirty-five households in Howbert and a population of 73; ten years later, there wasn't much change. There were twenty-nine households with a population of 70. Even though the trains were long gone, the population grew in 1930 to 107 residents in thirty-one households.

But maybe it was lively. In Harry C. Epperson's book, he wrote about growing up in Howbert. A son of Hardy and Josephine Epperson, he was born about 1880. He said, "Two women lived down by the railroad bridge, their cheeks were painted red and their hair was [dyed] yellow."

As a child, Harry Epperson was curious about the two women. He said, "I often wondered, as a boy, why all of the other women went into a whispering huddle whenever these women entered the stores, and why they didn't attend any of the neighborhood dances or parties."

PARTIES

And there were parties in Howbert. One was after the November 1888 election. The citizens of Howbert "enjoyed a grand barbecue at which

Epperson Annual Ball, November 8, 1899. *Park County Local History Archives, Harry C. Epperson Estate.*

whole beeves and mutton were served and consumed and the whole neighborhood participated in a grand dance in the evening," the November 22, 1888 *Flume* reported. The reason for the celebration was the result of an election bet.

The story didn't say who lost the bet and paid for the town party, and one can only speculate on what the election bet may have been. But it could have had something to do with the close race in the presidential election. In 1888, Grover Cleveland, the Democratic incumbent, won the popular vote by a slim margin yet lost the election in the Electoral College to his Republican opponent, Benjamin Harrison. (Ironically, four years later, the tables were turned and Cleveland was elected over Harrison.)

The town also had an annual ball. A photo donated to the Park County Local History Archives from the Harry C. Epperson Estate has a caption: "Howbert, 1899, Epperson annual ball." The photo shows a group of about fifty people outside on a porch dressed in their best. It appears the "annual ball" was attended by just about everyone in town.

MINING

Not all of the mining in Park County was along the Continental Divide. The March 17, 1892 *Flume* said there "seems to be quite a mining boom" in the foothills south of Howbert and Spinney (a town five and a half miles west of Howbert, now gone).

It said that "there is a mysterious whisper going of valuable discoveries already made, but we have no authentic intelligence." But it did report an increased interest in picking up area property on delinquent tax liens.

The newspaper may have been referring to a boom at the Freshwater Mining District (now Guffey), sixteen miles south of Freshwater Station.

Later that year, in July, *The Flume* reported three placer claims had been filed "on ground lying between Howbert and the Eleven Mile Canon." (*Canon* is the typical late 1800s spelling of *canyon*.)

One wonders if that was the reason why "the Cripple Creek people" were "agitating strongly" to form a new county by merging parts of Park, Fremont and El Paso Counties, as reported in the January 12, 1893 *Flume*. For Park County, the deal would have cut about 270 square miles from its southeastern corner.

That takeover would have included the area around Howbert, Eleven Mile Canyon, the future site of Eleven Mile Reservoir State Park, a small portion of the future Lost Creek Wilderness and a portion of Tarryall Road from U.S. 24 up to a point midway between the Ute Creek Trailhead and Twin Eagles Campground, where Allen Creek crosses the road, or all points "east of Range 73 and south of Township 10," *The Flume* said.

It would have taken twelve and a half miles of Midland Railroad track. That property alone, worth $9,124 per mile, would have resulted in a loss of $114,050 to Park County.

The Flume reported that "probably one-tenth of our taxable property would be taken from us, and that is a matter that interests everyone in the county."

But it didn't happen. When Teller County was finally formed in March 1899, Park County did not give up any land, and Teller was formed from parts of El Paso and Fremont Counties.

NOT ALL GOOD

It may have been a good life at Howbert, but it wasn't all good. The nearest doctors and law enforcement were forty miles away at Fairplay. People in the vicinity of Howbert had to take care of things on their own.

In December 1889, *The Flume* reported "eight cases of typhus fever and pneumonia in Howbert." Three of the eight were reported to be severely ill, and one, a Mr. Hunter, also had suffered a "paralytic stroke." (Typhus fever is a bacterial infection and is spread by the bites of lice, fleas and ticks. The most common in Colorado is tick-borne typhus fever, or Rocky Mountain spotted fever. But a person is unlikely to be bitten by a tick during a South Park winter. Another form of typhus fever is spread by lice in winter months, when people are mostly indoors, living in close quarters.)

In September 1890, a gunfight in Hammond's Saloon in Howbert left one man, William Langley, seriously wounded. *The Flume* reported, "[He] is said to have a fair chance of recovery." Langley's brother George Langley came up from Colorado Springs to attend to his wounded brother.

But soon after arriving in Howbert, George Langley was fatally injured when he ran directly at a Midland train engine that was speeding through Howbert and was "horribly mangled." He died within an hour.

A newspaper story in September 1890 reported, "The theory is that he had become insane from excitement and deliberately committed suicide."

In May 1894, Father John Dyer, then age eighty-two, was accidently thrown from a vehicle while traveling from religious services at Balfour. He was cared for at the Robbins family home at Howbert. Dyer recovered and lived another seven years; he died on June 16, 1901, at age eighty-nine.

Accidents happen, and one four miles east of Howbert on August 27, 1915, seriously injured thirty-three passengers on an eastbound Colorado Midland train returning from a "Wildflower Special" excursion. The Midland ran daily summer excursions from Colorado City to the town of Spinney, stopping along the way so passengers could take photographs and gather wildflowers. The eastbound crew was given orders at the Howbert station to wait at Idlewild (three and a half miles east of Howbert) until a westbound train passed. For whatever reason, the eastbound didn't wait, and the two trains collided a half mile east of Idlewild.

The original investigative report dated September 16, 1915, which said the view of both engineers "was obscured by the almost perpendicular walls of the canon on the south side of the railroad," gives a hint of the accident location.

MIDLAND SHUTS DOWN

The Colorado Midland had an even shorter life than Howbert. It ran thirty-one years, until 1918. The tracks were dismantled in 1921, and a highway was built along the old rail bed. That was a blow to Howbert, but by then, transportation needs were shifting to motor vehicles, which had been mass produced since 1912.

The town held on for another fifteen years, until 1933.

HOWBERT'S END

But population growth in Colorado's capital affected the citizens of Howbert. In the first part of the twentieth century, the City and County of Denver began looking for more water sources; that search lingered on South Park. By 1926, its Board of Water Commissioners decided on the Eleven Mile site and started survey work for the Eleven Mile Canyon Dam.

In October 2012, the former site of Howbert, Colorado, is buried under the waters of Eleven Mile Reservoir at Eleven Mile State Park. *Author photo.*

Construction of the dam started in 1930 and was completed in 1932.

The town of Howbert was still alive on April 10, 1933, when a special meeting was called by the Howbert school district. The meeting was to decide where to move the Howbert schoolhouse and "also to authorize the school board to spend the necessary money to move said building to [a] new location. [And] also to [authorize the school board to] purchase the necessary ground for [the] same," according to a notice posted by Alice Jones, secretary of Park County School District Number 6.

Later in 1933, the last of the property that was to become Eleven Mile Reservoir was purchased by Denver. Gradually, the South Platte River flooded Howbert, Idlewild, Freshwater Station and some of the nearby ranches. An extension on the dam in 1957 buried more ranch land and eventually brought the reservoir's capacity to 97,779 acre-feet of water. (An acre-foot is the volume of water that will cover an area of one acre to a depth of one foot.)

1890s

Chapter 12

GOTTLIEB FLUHMANN

Disappeared from Lake George Area in 1892; Remains,
Including Valuable Possessions, Discovered in
Remote Cave in 1944

In life, Gottlieb Fluhmann passed through Park County history a forgotten man. But that changed with the discovery of Fluhmann's remains and worldly possessions in a secret hideaway in the hills northwest of Lake George, Colorado, fifty-two years after he went missing.

Fluhmann disappeared from his Lake George–area ranch sometime in the fall of 1892. His remains and that of an animal, possibly a pet dog, along with some valuable worldly possessions, were found by chance when two army air corps GIs from Peterson Field (now Peterson Air Force Base, Colorado Springs) went hiking in the area northwest of Lake George in the fall of 1944.

The Tarryall Valley near Lake George, Colorado, as it looked in the early 1900s when Gottlieb Fluhmann disappeared from the area. *Park County Local History Archives, Wilkin Collection.*

One of the men, Master Sergeant Francis Brahler, climbed to the top of a large granite formation to get his bearings. Window glass reflecting from the sun caught Brahler's eye. He discovered that the window glass could slide to one side.

And when he slid the glass, Brahler discovered Fluhmann's Cave.

Fluhmann

Fluhmann's last venture was ranching, but he had also worked as a land surveyor and a miner. He was born in Switzerland in about 1837 and immigrated to the United States in the early 1860s, according to documentation on his passport found in the cave after his death. He was five feet, four inches tall and was counted in the June 1880 U.S. census as a rancher in South Park, Park County, Colorado. He was about fifty-five when he disappeared in 1892.

According to the November 2, 1944 Colorado Springs *Gazette Telegraph*, Fluhmann "was of a 'flighty' temperament and troubled by the thought that someone was stealing his cattle periodically."

The *Fairplay Flume* of that date said Fluhmann "was quick to pick up imaginary insult or attempt to cheat him" and that he had frequent altercations with "some of the old timers."

However, in considering the personality traits attributed to Fluhmann, one must remember that they were written fifty-two years after Fluhmann's death by those whose memories may have clouded or by those who didn't know Fluhmann at all.

The *Gazette* said Fluhmann had angry words with several cattlemen, including Benjamin Ratcliff, who ranched near Jefferson in the Tarryall Valley. Ratcliff murdered three school board members in 1895 and was hanged at the state penitentiary in Cañon City for his crime.

Ratcliff Connection

In the months and years following the Fluhmann Cave discovery, legends reported as truth circulated in publications of the day speculating that Benjamin Ratcliff was Fluhmann's murderer.

But the 1944 stories included several inaccurate details that should have been simple to confirm, such as Ratcliff's physical appearance and the names, ages and genders of his children.

With the simplest details incorrect, one tends to question the accuracy of any part of the story.

But it wasn't the first time Ratcliff was suspected of the murder. The first speculation surfaced in May 1895, within days after Ratcliff was charged with the school board murders.

One of the early publications was the May 15, 1895 Buena Vista–based *Colorado Democrat*. In that article, Fluhmann was described as a "well-to-do ranchman" who left behind a "fine ranch and a thousand head of cattle."

The 1,000-head figure may be another inaccuracy; the administrator of Fluhmann's estate, Henry Krebill, sold 150 head on April 6, 1893, to a Kansas City party and another 16 head in the final estate sale on May 11, 1893.

Reasons given for naming Ratcliff as Fluhmann's murderer were that the two could not agree on a cattle deal, and soon after that, Fluhmann disappeared, after which Ratcliff "appeared to be uneasy and [had] always been heavily armed," according to the *Colorado Democrat* story.

Ratcliff was not considered a suspect in 1892 when Fluhmann disappeared, and he was never charged with Fluhmann's murder.

There was speculation in 1944 that other possibilities of Fluhmann's fate could be death from natural causes, suffocation from a warming or cooking fire without adequate ventilation or suicide.

THE CAVE

The cave is more a crevice in the rock than an actual cave. The entrance is not visible from ground level; a second entryway, on the roof of the cave, is visible only from the top of the rocky outcropping, according to newspaper stories published in 1944 in *The Flume*, the *Gazette* and the *Greeley Daily Tribune*.

Michael Anthony, an employee at the M Lazy C Ranch near Lake George in 2012, has been to the cave. He said that "[in 2012] there is no evidence of a door, but the opening is configured to look like a door could easily be built to fit."

He said the cave is small, about fifteen feet deep, five feet high and five feet wide. "It has a flat floor and the sides are straight up and down. It's just made up of native rock; there is an opening in the ceiling next to the wall where it looked like he could put his stove pipe," said Anthony.

Home

Fluhmann had fashioned the one-room cave into a home.

The November 2, 1944 *Gazette* said that a huge dishpan hung from beams in the rocky ceiling. In the pan were two loaded, gold-inlaid, double-barreled flintlock rifles; a .45-caliber pistol; and "expensive smoking pipes." Also in the dishpan was a surveyor's transit, which included a telescope that was "perfectly preserved and operable," according to the *Gazette*.

There were letters Fluhmann had received a few years earlier from John Fluhmann, a nephew then living in Crested Butte, Colorado, and Alice Fluhmann, a niece from Missouri. There were legal papers and his Swiss passport.

The cave had a wooden floor, and shelving was attached to the wall to hold Fluhmann's possessions. Among those were shoes, a Dutch oven, several wine bottles, a brown jug, a two-gallon crock and "expensive wood working tools," said the *Gazette*. A kerosene lamp, with fuel that still burned after fifty-two years, was also found.

Another Gun

Fluhmann had one other gun in the cave. It was an 1886 Marlin repeater .38-.55- caliber rifle. That rifle, in good shape, would sell for approximately $1,500 to $2,600 in the early 2010s, according to information found at www.collectorebooks.com.

But Fluhmann's rifle was not in good shape.

Its stock was bullet-damaged, and the barrel was rusted. It was found in the middle of the cave next to Fluhmann's skull. Reported in the *Gazette* story was that then Park County sheriff Sylvester Law said if a right-handed person was holding the gun and preparing to shoot when the bullet from another gun hit the rifle stock, that person would be killed.

Speculation at the time was that Fluhmann could have been shot from the hole in the top of his cave. But newspaper reports from 1944 did not mention bullet holes on Fluhmann's skull or on the rest of his skeleton. Reports did, however, mention that no stray bullet was found.

And Dan Denney (or Denny) from Fairplay, who was a twelve-year-old child when Fluhmann disappeared and who knew Fluhmann in the 1890s, was among those who investigated the cave in 1944. He said that he "talked to men who had seen Fluhmann carrying the rifle with the damaged stock sometime before he disappeared."

Left Home

Fluhmann didn't always live in the cave. He could view his homestead—with its two cabins, assortment of sheds and corrals and herd of cattle—from the cave entrance. His home was in a narrow valley with a good supply of water and plenty of grazing land.

Speculation is that he used the surveyor's transit to get a better view of the homestead and of anyone who might be looking for him. It was the disappearance of the surveying instrument from the homestead that led Fluhmann's neighbors to consider that he may have left the area.

A few short paragraphs in the January 12, 1893 *Flume* said that Tim Borden—Fluhmann's neighbor and a resident of Bordenville northwest of the cave on present-day Tarryall Road—thought that with the surveying instrument missing, "there is a bare possibility that he has gone off to some of the new camps with it."

But the article continued, "The neighbors incline to the belief that he is dead, and that his death was accidental or suicide. He was a peculiar character and has been know[n] to talk of making away with himself."

Another story, in the April 20, 1893 *Flume*, said that Fluhmann had "remarked to different parties that he would kill himself" and that "when he did disappear they would never be able to find him."

But search parties did try to find him. Representatives from the sheriff's office and others scoured the area of Fluhmann's ranch in the months between February and April 1893, not knowing if they would find the missing man or his remains. Fluhmann's nephew, John Fluhmann, traveled to Park County from his home in Crested Butte, Colorado, to join in the search.

No trace of Fluhmann was found during the 1893 searches.

POSSESSIONS

The items found in the cave had some monetary value, but after all the passing years, it is unknown what happened to most of Fluhmann's possessions. The November 2, 1944 *Flume* said, "The debris has been well sorted and gleaned [gathered] by the Sheriff and his helpers."

But it is known what happened to one of Fluhmann's guns.

One of the 1850s-era gold-inlaid flintlock rifles was bought in 1973 by the wife of Bill Blunt, a forester with the Pike National Forest stationed in Fairplay. After extensive research on its historic and monetary value, she bought the rifle from an unidentified private individual in Fairplay as a birthday gift for her husband, according to the February 25, 1973 *Gazette*.

The gun is rare, but a current value could not be determined.

UNKNOWN

In 1976, an inventory data form, filed in the Park County Local History Archives, was completed for the Gottlieb Fluhmann Cave. The form gives a short description of Fluhmann and lists articles that were found in the cave in 1944. The report, signed by the late Park County historian Harold Warren, said, "He could have died of natural causes or from a bullet which plowed through the stock of his 1886 Model .38 caliber Marlin rifle.

"To this day, no one really knows what happened to him."

Chapter 13

THE SHORT, TRAGIC LIFE OF
ANNA BLYTHE SPEAS

Belle of Boulder, Suspected Criminal in Como,
Dead in Denver at Twenty-eight

There are very few people living who have experienced riding the narrow-gauge railroad through Platte Canyon into South Park. The last passenger train left Como in April 1937, and in the years from 1879 until the railroad shut down, trains were the modern way to travel in Park County.

Some rode the rails to the city to visit old friends or for cultural activities that were not available in small mountain towns. Others may have taken a trip back home to bury a loved one.

But not many were riding the train escorted by the sheriff; not many had a court date to be tried as an accessory to murder.

Anna Blythe Speas was an exception.

The Flume of May 17, 1894, said that on Tuesday, May 15, Sheriff Dan H. Wilson escorted Mrs. Anna Speas from Boulder in preparation for her trial, answering charges of "accessory to the killing of Town Marshal Cook, of Como, a few weeks ago." The story said that Mary Jane Blythe, Anna's mother, was with her. They were bound for court in Fairplay.

Interior of an 1890s' narrow-gauge passenger car. Anna Speas rode in a car like this back to Como for the murder trial. *Photo courtesy of the Tom Klinger Collection.*

BELLE OF BOULDER

There was a time, however, when Anna Speas's life was a young girl's dream.

Anna Blythe met Sam Speas in Boulder in 1884. He was one of the many railroaders who lived at the boardinghouse owned by Anna's mother and operated by Anna's sister Nellie and her husband, Joe McCabe, according to Anna's great-nephew, Rick Clapham. Anna served meals at the house.

Anna Blythe was the belle of Boulder; she was beautiful—tall and shapely with wavy black hair and deep aquamarine eyes, said Clapham. She was sought after by all the young men in town, according to Margaret Coel, the granddaughter of Sam Speas and the author of a book on Speas's life, *Goin' Railroading*.

Sam Speas, husband of Anna Blythe Speas. *Photo courtesy of Margaret Coel, S.F. Speas Collection.*

115

Anna, at age seventeen, probably had dreams of "happily ever after" when she married Speas on September 30, 1886.

MURDER OF THE MARSHAL

Less than eight years later, in 1894, Anna was caught in the middle of a murder investigation. The marshal of Como—Adolph E. Cook, more commonly called A.E.—was shot and killed at Levi Streeter's home in Como when he was investigating a loud party. Anna and her friend Lillian Robinson were there.

Streeter (also spelled Streetor and Streator) was charged with first-degree murder; Anna and Robinson were charged as accessories.

DEATH IN DENVER

Anna was acquitted of the crime, but two years later, she was dead—beaten repeatedly and left to die in Denver by men she might have considered friends.

MARRIAGE

During the two years between 1884 and 1886—while Anna was working in the Boulder boardinghouse and Speas worked for the Greeley, Salt Lake & Pacific Railroad out of Boulder—the two spent as much time together as they could. In summertime, they took long walks, went roller-skating and attended shows of traveling entertainers. In winter, they went sledding.

In 1886, they were married. They lived in Boulder for the next fourteen months. It was a town of about three thousand, with a fledgling new college housed all in one building, called "Old Main," the beginnings of the University of Colorado.

In November 1887, Sam Speas was promoted to engineer with the Denver, South Park & Pacific Railroad and transferred to Como.

FIRST ARRIVAL IN COMO

The first time Anna Speas arrived in Como on the train, she was eighteen years old. Her husband was the tall, handsome, redheaded Sam Speas. At twenty-nine, he was eleven years her senior and destined to become one of the highest-ranking engineers in the Como yard.

Sam had arrived a few weeks before Anna and bought a home in Como next to the Dunbar Livery. He was waiting for Anna on the depot platform that November day to take her to their new home.

The Pacific Hotel, Anna's first sight on arrival in Como, Colorado, in November 1887. The hotel burned to the ground in 1896. *George Mellen photograph from the Ed and Nancy Bathke Collection.*

LIFE IN COMO

Sam Speas loved Como. From the moment he first saw South Park from the Kenosha Station, he knew that Como was the place he wanted to stay. His career as a railroad engineer was thriving. Como was a busy thoroughfare,

Anna Speas left a note in high school student Alice Holthusen's autograph book in January 1890. *Photo courtesy of Diana Copsey.*

and engineers were the railroad aristocracy, looked up to and admired by almost everyone in town.

Speas ran freight trains in his first years as an engineer, and in that job, each time he reported at the roundhouse for work, he never knew where he was going or when he would be home. That lack of routine was a big attraction to railroad men. They liked living on the edge, the feeling of not knowing what lay around the next curve in the track. It was an adventurous life, according to Coel's book.

The women in Como were left behind to take care of the routine chores. They chopped firewood, shoveled snow, milked cows, cared for the children and made repairs to homes. And when a train pulled into town, they had meals ready—at any hour of the day or night—for their returning men. They worked the long hours that the men did, but without the adventure and excitement that riding the train afforded.

Anna may have had a hard time fitting in with life in Como. She was young, perhaps younger than the wives of the other railroad men. She spent time with some of the high school girls, but she didn't fit in with them either. Many young wives met other women through children's activities, but Anna had no children. Many young women made acquaintances through work, but Anna did not work in Como.

The infant children of Sam and Anna Speas share a deteriorating headstone in the Como Cemetery in a photo from 2011. *Author photo.*

Sam was Anna's anchor, but with him away much of the time, it seems likely that Anna was very lonely. During the seven years she lived in Como, Anna had three babies; they all died at birth or soon after. There is no way to know today, but there is a good chance that Sam Speas, because of his work schedule, was not home for the births and deaths of his children. His absence would have made the losses more heartbreaking for Anna.

And even today, the story of the Speas babies is heartbreaking. The only record of them is a shared deteriorating headstone in the Como Cemetery.

After the loss of her children, Anna Speas began drinking heavily, according to family stories. And she may have finally found her niche when she met others in town who shared that pastime, among them, Levi Streeter. He ran a shoe making and shoe repair service out of his home. Another acquaintance was Lillian Kennedy Robinson, the other identified woman at the party where Cook was shot.

(Robinson's husband divorced her during the trial. Her surname was changed to Kennedy halfway through the trial transcripts, and she is now referred to as Kennedy in this story.)

Como Crime

It was Friday, April 6, 1894, when Cook lost his life.

The Flume of April 12, 1894, reported Cook went to Streeter's home about midnight to investigate a loud party. Anna Speas and Kennedy were in the home. *The Flume* reported that there might have been two other men and another woman present, but it was never confirmed. Both women testified there were no others at Streeter's home that night.

According to Streeter's story, a man knocked on the door and ordered Streeter to hold up his hands. Streeter said he thought he was about to be robbed. He opened the door and, without hesitation, began firing his gun at the marshal who was standing on the doorstep. Three bullets hit Cook, two in the head and one in the chest. After the shooting, Streeter beat Cook's head with the handle of the revolver, cracking his skull. Cook died instantly.

There was speculation at the time that Streeter thought it was Sam Speas at the door and that Streeter feared being caught with Mrs. Speas in his house.

Anna testified she never heard a knock on the door, but she said Kennedy told her someone was knocking. When Streeter answered the door, both women broke a window and went out the back. They cut themselves on broken glass, and authorities were able to trace a blood trail to the Speas home.

Anna Speas told investigators, "I went down to Mr. Streeter's after my shoe which was there to be fixed." She said, in her signed statement, that she and "Lill Kennedy" went out the window because "we wanted to go home and Streeter didn't want us to go." She said she did not drink anything at Streeter's house.

Kennedy told a slightly different story. She said the two went to Streeter's house about 9:00 p.m., stayed for about an hour and had no particular reason to go there. She said, "We drank whiskey with Mr. Streeter." But she said they were not intoxicated.

Kennedy wrote in a statement, "We could not get [the] door unlocked and broke [a] window out. When we were breaking [the] window we heard Mr. Streeter talking to somebody and were afraid somebody would come in and see us."

The story on the front page of the April 12, 1894 *Flume* gives the impression of much larger party at Streeter's house that night:

> *On the night in question a little party of men and women, of doubtful character to say the least, were holding a jollification at Streeter's place, finally becoming quite convivial* [sociable] *and noisy through partaking of frequent draughts of beer. It is believed that there were present at the time three women and two men besides the proprietor of the place, though but two of the women are as yet known, these being Mrs. Anna Speas, whose husband was temporarily absent in Denver, and Mrs. Lillie Robinson. Suspicion attaches to another woman and also to two men, it is said, as the last mentioned were seen running away from the direction of the house after the shooting.*

Evidence uncovered during the research of this story shows that Sam Speas may not have been "absent in Denver" at the time of the party at Streeter's home. His railroad time sheets for that time period are in possession of the family, and they show he was not working between April 4 and April 11, 1894. If Sam Speas was in Como on the evening of April 6, Streeter very well could have believed Speas was the man knocking on the door.

MARSHAL ADOLPH E. COOK

Cook had been marshal of Como since at least October 1887. He had just been elected to another term on April 3, 1894—three days before he was murdered. He had lived in Como since at least the fall of 1884. An article in the November 5, 1884 *Como Headlight* mentioned his presence at a masquerade ball on Thursday, October 29, of that year. He dressed as a cowboy.

He was prominent in railroad circles and had previously worked as foreman of the South Park railroad shops in Como, where he was in charge of the section of the work force that repaired engines, cars and snowplows. He was a member of the Independent Order of Odd Fellows (IOOF) and the Knights of Pythias and was about forty-five years old at the time of his death. He lived in Como with his wife and three daughters; the eldest was then twelve years old. *The Flume* of April 12, 1894, reported that he "was a quiet and well-liked official."

"There was no known trouble between the two men [Cook and Streeter]," it said.

LEVI J. STREETER

Streeter had lived in Como since at least December 1890. He was described in the April 12, 1894 *Flume* as "a single man, and if reports be true, has borne none to savory a reputation in Como where he has lived for several years and carried on business." Among residents there he was considered "somewhat flighty at times, but not dangerous." In another part of the same *Flume* edition, it was said that Streeter "was considered a peaceable man."

Streeter lived in a two-room house; one room was used for living quarters, and one room was used for his business of shoe making and repair.

Colorado State Penitentiary mugshot of Levi J. Streeter. *Colorado State Archives photo*.

TRIAL

Anna Speas, Kennedy and Streeter were taken to the Fairplay jail after the murder. The women were confined in the stone jail on the courthouse lawn for at least one night but later were allowed free on bond until the trial in May 1894. Streeter stayed in jail until the trial.

Sam Speas supported his wife throughout the trial and hired the most prosperous attorney in Park County, Webster Ballinger of Como, for her defense. Ironically, Ballinger was also the court-appointed attorney for Streeter.

Both women were found not guilty.

Streeter was convicted of murder in the first degree and sentenced to hang in June 1894 at Cañon City. His sentence was later changed to "imprisonment for life, hard labor," which didn't buy him much time. He died in prison on April 9, 1896, of consumption (tuberculosis), according to Colorado State Penitentiary records.

AFTER THE TRIAL

Even after being found not guilty, Anna Speas's life was never the same. At the age of twenty-five, she left Como on the train as soon as the trial was over. She never returned.

To get order back in his life, Sam Speas went to court and divorced Anna on the grounds of drunkenness and cruelty on July 10, 1894. His attorney, Ballinger, was with him, but Anna was not in court.

And Sam Speas went on with his life. On October 29, 1895, he married Ellen O'Leary, who worked at the Pacific Hotel. They raised three boys, all of whom followed their father's profession and became railroad engineers.

Anna went back to Boulder and later moved to Denver and continued to drink heavily, according to Coel. In Denver, she met and moved in with Andrew Lyles, a black man who lived in a shack near Twenty-first and Lawrence Streets. Lyles mistreated Anna and often beat her. Her mother begged her to come home to Boulder, but Anna refused.

And then her life deteriorated further. On the night of July 5, 1898, Lyles had "beaten her into insensibility," according to testimony by neighbors. They said they heard the beating going on all night. Anna died in the morning.

Lyles and John C. Motley, another man who lived in the home, were arrested and charged with Anna's murder, but even in that violent death, it appears Anna may not have gotten justice. The men were cleared of murder charges when the autopsy report said she died of internal abscess, pneumonia and alcoholism—not specifically from the beating.

Lyles was rearrested the same day on another charge, criminal assault on a six-year-old girl.

Anna Blythe Speas died alone on July 6, 1898, in a rundown Denver shack. Less than twelve years had elapsed from a young woman's dreams of "happily ever after" to death at the hands of supposed friends. She was twenty-eight years old.

She is buried in an unmarked grave at Fairmount Cemetery in Denver.

National Law Enforcement Memorial

More than a century after his murder, Como marshal A.E. Cook was inducted into the National Law Enforcement Memorial at the Twenty-third Annual Candlelight Vigil during National Police Week in Washington, D.C., on May 13, 2011. He was similarly inducted into the Colorado Law Enforcement Memorial in May 1999. The memorials honor officers killed in the line of duty. Cook is still, in 2013, the only law enforcement officer from Park County to qualify.

Chapter 14

BENJAMIN RATCLIFF

Park County Pioneer, Civil War Veteran, Triple Murderer;
What Happened and Why

On May 6, 1895, Benjamin Ratcliff, a homesteader in the Tarryall area, rode his horse to the Michigan Creek School about seven miles southeast of Jefferson, dismounted, walked into the schoolhouse and shot three members of the school board.

Lincoln F. McCurdy and Samuel Taylor died instantly; George Douglas Wyatt lived four more painful hours. Wyatt's signed deathbed statement read, "Ratcliff claimed that we had slandered him."

Ratcliff confessed and turned himself in at Como to Deputy James Link and was escorted to jail in Fairplay.

Found in his pocket at the time of arrest was a letter to Ratcliff from neighbor Susan Crockett telling him of a rumor begun by school board member Lincoln F. McCurdy, who said that one of Ratcliff's daughters was six months pregnant. Crockett did not specifically say in her letter, but it was revealed at trial that the rumor alleged that Ratcliff was the father of the unborn child.

The schoolhouse is long gone, but legends and rumors of the Ratcliff tragedy live on, clouding the truth.

Colorado State Penitentiary mugshot of Benjamin Ratcliff. *Colorado State Archives photo.*

CIVIL WAR SERVICE

Ratcliff was twenty years old in 1861 when Park County became one of the seventeen original counties in the then Colorado Territory. On April 12, 1861, when the Southern states fired on Fort Sumter to begin the Civil War, Ratcliff began preparing to join the Union army.

He enlisted in Missouri, and his assignment was wagon master in the quartermaster's department, the unit that specializes in distributing supplies and provisions to troops. Ratcliff fought in the Battle of Shiloh (Tennessee) in April 1862. Following the Union victory at Shiloh, the Confederate army was pursued into Mississippi. In the surge, Ratcliff's horse fell and rolled on his legs and hips, causing permanent and painful injury, according to testimony provided by Ratcliff at his murder trial.

Ratcliff fought in the Battle of Lexington (Missouri) and was captured by Confederate forces on October 19, 1864, when he was acting as a scout for General Pleasanton. He escaped two days later, on his twenty-third birthday, and spent the rest of the war on duty in the Jefferson City, Missouri area.

PARK COUNTY PIONEER

In June 1871, Ratcliff, twenty-nine, married neighbor Elizabeth McNair, thirty-five, in Montieau County, Missouri. That fall, the newlyweds took the train to Denver, a stagecoach to Colorado Springs and traveled probably by wagon or horseback from Colorado Springs to the Tarryall area, according to the book *The Legend of Benjamin Ratcliff* by Chris O. Andrew, a great-grandson of Ratcliff.

The Homestead Act of 1862 provided for the transfer of 160 acres of unoccupied public land to each homesteader in payment of a nominal fee after five years of residence. The Ratcliffs homesteaded in the upper Tarryall region between Jefferson and the current site of Tarryall Reservoir. The property grew into a successful ranching operation that stayed in the family for thirty years. By 1885, Ratcliff reported for the Colorado census that he owned four horses, twenty head of milk cows, thirty head of other cattle, twenty calves born, forty-nine additional calves bought, twenty-five cattle slaughtered, 1,225 unmowed acres and 65 mowed acres, which produced 150 tons of hay. The ranch also produced six hundred pounds of butter.

The former homestead is interspersed with rolling hills and is hidden from prying eyes by stands of pine and aspen trees. When I visited the site in June 2011, the bottomlands where Ratcliff must have cut hay had trickling streams and soggy areas of cool, clear water. Surrounding pastures were edged with large rock formations, covered with wildflowers and native grasses and dotted with badger holes.

The deteriorating two-room cabin had no roof and no windows. Two tiny rabbits, no bigger than a man's hand, were hiding in the fallen timbers and had apparently taken up residence. Walls were, for the most part,

Former Ratcliff homestead near Jefferson, Colorado, in June 2011. *Author photo.*

intact and amazingly sturdy after 140 years of assault by South Park wind and weather.

The feel of the place, when sitting next to the cabin ruin, is one of peacefulness, but one could easily imagine a lingering sadness from the events the family endured in 1882, when Ratcliff's wife died, and in 1895, when the murders happened.

ELIZABETH DIES

Elizabeth Ratcliff was pregnant with her fourth child in October 1882 when she and the baby died in childbirth at the family ranch. Their shared grave is at the Bordenville Cemetery near the former town site of the same name on Tarryall Road. Benjamin was left a widower at age forty-one with three young children to raise: Howell, almost eight; Lizzie, five; and Lavina, or Vina, four.

Probably feeling overwhelmed with taking care of the ranch and three young children, Ratcliff sent the two girls back to Missouri to live with relatives in about September 1884. Howell stayed on the ranch and took on adult responsibilities early, without his mother, with his sisters far away in Missouri and saddled with the job of helping his father run the ranch. Sometime between 1892 and 1894, Lizzie and Vina returned to the family ranch to live. Lizzie would have been between fifteen and seventeen and Vina between fourteen and sixteen. Howell was between eighteen and twenty.

Important to the story is that Lizzie had a severe limp from an injury that occurred either shortly before she left home for Missouri or while she was in Missouri. She had fallen off a chair and broken her hip. Evidently, she was not seen by a doctor. When the hip healed, it left one leg about six inches shorter than the other.

LEADING UP TO MURDER

Letters written between Ratcliff and Superintendent of Schools George Miller and also between Ratcliff and his neighbor and Secretary of the School Board Samuel Taylor indicate that Ratcliff was frustrated with the school board.

The Ratcliff homestead was about six miles by road from the Michigan Creek School. School was held only during the winter months because children had to be home helping with ranch chores during the rest of the year. The journey to school was a hardship to the Ratcliff children and especially Lizzie. She could not mount or ride a horse easily or run or walk long distances. Ratcliff's request of the school board was that the school be located closer to his ranch or a teacher be sent out to his ranch, or if those requests couldn't be fulfilled, he asked to be allowed to borrow the schoolbooks in the off-season so that he could teach his children at home. Ratcliff mentioned in his letters that other ranchers had been allowed to borrow the schoolbooks in the off-season.

Ratcliff was continuously denied permission to borrow the books. He wrote to Miller on June 8, 1894, asking if records were kept showing that the school owned the textbooks. In testimony at trial, Ratcliff implied that if the books were owned by the school, then taxpayers should have access to them because the school was supported by taxes.

Miller replied to Ratcliff the very next day, saying that he (Miller) was new to the job and, regarding ownership of textbooks, that the previous superintendent, "whoever he was[,] at that time should have kept a record of same. If not and the district is damaged by his neglect he is liable." As for why others had been able to borrow books while Ratcliff was being denied the privilege, Miller said, "I am sure I don't know why there should be a difference made between your children and others." Ratcliff became more frustrated by Miller's prompt but empty reply.

A few months later, on August 16, 1894, something happened that probably made Ratcliff even angrier. Two itinerant workers showed up at Ratcliff's homestead. Ratcliff hired them but "didn't like the appearance of the men," as Ratcliff testified at his trial. He thought they were acting strangely and eavesdropped on one of their conversations. He overheard the two discussing the ten dollars they could earn by telling McCurdy that one of Ratcliff's daughters was pregnant. The person paying the itinerants was identified at trial only by the last name Crosier.

There was a member of the Michigan Creek school board named E.R. Crosier. There was also a Crosier who held one of the earliest water rights on the upper Tarryall Creek. Whether they were one and the same was not discovered.

Ratcliff was eccentric, and it came out in the trial that he would put up fences on his property so that neighbors could not get to the water sources of the upper Tarryall.

On August 22, 1894, Ratcliff received the Crockett letter telling about McCurdy's statement, which was made at a school board of directors meeting, that one of Ratcliff's daughters was pregnant. Crockett explained in her letter, "I think it is right you should know." Neither of Ratcliff's daughters was pregnant.

Ratcliff, who had the letter in his pocket on the day of the murders, testified at his trial that he went to the school to see if the school board members would plead guilty to his charges of libel and slander related to the rumors McCurdy was spreading about his daughter. If not, he said he was going to Fairplay to file charges.

At the trial, Dr. C.H. Scott of Como, one of the physicians who responded to the Michigan Creek School after the shootings, heard the last words of the dying Wyatt. Scott said Wyatt quoted Ratcliff as saying before the shootings began, "You folks have slandered me, have accused me of being intimate with my own daughter."

Ratcliff knew the school board was meeting that day because Miller had told him. Miller and the fifth board member, Crosier, were delayed and didn't make it to the 10:00 a.m. meeting that Monday.

Ratcliff walked into the schoolhouse carrying a .38 pocket pistol and an 1873 Winchester, according to court testimony by Park County sheriff's deputy James Link.

Wyatt said as he was dying that Ratcliff fired his .44 Winchester accidently and that the ball went into the floor at Taylor's feet. There was "excited discussion," said Wyatt, during which Ratcliff raised his gun and shot Taylor in the face, killing him instantly. Next he shot McCurdy in the back; he also died instantly.

He shot Wyatt in the hips; Wyatt lived about four hours longer.

Immediately after the shootings, Ratcliff left the school and headed his horse toward Fairplay. He met Deputy Link on the road and told Link he shot McCurdy when McCurdy rushed at him, according to testimony at the trial. Ratcliff traveled by horseback onto Como's Rowe Street with Link following in a wagon.

It was not until their arrival in Como that Link took custody of Ratcliff and disarmed him. Ratcliff climbed into the back of Link's wagon and together they turned toward Fairplay, where they were met by Sheriff D.H. Wilson at Trout Creek, two miles southeast of Como.

Trial, Sentencing, Execution

Ratcliff was first taken to Fairplay, but fear of lynching caused a transfer to the Chaffee County jail in Salida, where a trial was held in July 1895. Ratcliff was found guilty of premeditated murder and sentenced to death by hanging.

After the verdict, Ratcliff bid "his motherless girls an affectionate farewell" but refused to take notice of his son, Howell, "who on the witness stand said he disapproved of his father's method of revenge on his family's slanderers," said a report in the July 27, 1895 *Aspen Weekly Times*.

The sentence was affirmed by the Colorado Supreme Court in January 1896 and was carried out at the penitentiary in Cañon City on February 7, 1896, despite a last-minute failed appeal to Governor Albert McIntyre by Ratcliff's lawyer, who claimed that his client was insane.

Ratcliff's body was returned by train from Cañon City to Buena Vista, where it lay on the dock for two days waiting for the next train to Como. Prisons didn't have a surplus of coffins; they used the same one over and over. The family—or possibly just his son, Howell—would have had to transfer the body to another coffin and send the penitentiary's property back.

Burial couldn't have been easy in February in frozen ground. A marker for Ratcliff is on his former homestead within a mile of the family's former home, now within the boundaries of Pike National Forest. It is at the base of a hill with views of South Park and the surrounding mountains. However, while it is believed by his descendants that Ratcliff is buried on the former homestead, there is some question on whether the marker is on the exact location of his burial.

Chapter 15

BOOM AND BUST ON BROSS

When Silver Reigned: 1868–93

It was on March 9, 1869, that Daniel Plummer and Joseph Myers, both of Alma, filed claim on the first silver mine on Mount Bross northwest of Alma, Colorado. They called it the Dwight.

The adjoining property—the Moose Mine—on which Plummer and Myers filed two years later, was the most productive in Park County, according to an 1880 book by Frank Fossett, *Colorado: Its Gold and Silver Mines, Farms and Stock Ranges and Health and Pleasure Resorts; Tourist's Guide to the Rocky Mountains*.

Plummer first arrived in Park County in July 1865 and settled in Montgomery. He was superintendent of the Pioneer Mill there.

Myers was a native of Pennsylvania and an 1860s Park County pioneer. He lived in Montgomery and Buckskin before settling in Fairplay, according to his obituary in the June 4, 1897 *Flume*. He became a trustee on the Fairplay town board on April 2, 1880.

Both Myers and Plummer had been searching for a rich discovery; they found it at the Moose in 1871 on the 13,600-foot level of Mount Bross.

DOLLY VARDEN

The Dolly Varden Mine, also on Mount Bross and discovered in 1872, "ranks next to the Moose in production and size of deposits and often surpasses that mine in richness of ore," Fossett said.

Dolly Varden mine in July 2011. *Photo courtesy of Christie Wright, taken with the owner's permission.*

It was discovered by George Brunk and Assyria "Cy" Hall in 1872. Before arriving in the Alma area, Brunk was working in Central City, Colorado, as a miner and teamster. When he heard about the Moose discovery, he moved his family to Park County. In July 1871, he teamed up with Hall.

Hall had been living in the Buckskin area since 1860, the beginning of the gold rush days. He was an owner of other gold and silver mines in both Park and Pitkin Counties. In 1870, he was Park County sheriff, according to the book *Mining Among the Clouds* by Harvey N. Gardiner, and in April 1879, he was elected to the Fairplay town board, as reported in the April 3, 1879 *Flume*.

The two discovered other mines on Bross, both separately and together, but it was their joint discovery of the Dolly Varden that made them rich, Gardiner said in his book.

1868 SILVER VALUE

Silver was first discovered on Mount Bross in 1868. At that time, the U.S. currency was based on a standard of both silver and gold and had been since 1837. One ounce of gold was equal in value to sixteen ounces of silver.

During the Civil War years, very little silver was mined, and the open-market price went up. Silver miners sold to jewelry makers and other silver users instead of to the government. That made the silver on Mount Bross highly valued. And because the silver ore ran horizontally and was not far beneath the ground's shale surface on a layer of limestone, it was relatively easy and inexpensive to mine.

The problem was getting the silver to market.

SMELTERS IN COLORADO

There was a smelter in Colorado in 1872, the Boston and Colorado Smelter in Black Hawk, which opened in 1868. But in the days before railroads or even decent wagon roads between Mount Bross and Black Hawk, it was difficult to get the ore to the smelter. The choices were to haul it by burros over Hoosier Pass, take it over Handcart Pass (near Webster) and then over

One route for getting ore to the smelter in Black Hawk was over Hoosier Pass, shown here in 1906. *Park County Local History Archives, Harold Sanborn postcard, South Park Historical Foundation.*

Argentine Pass to Black Hawk or take it to Denver and from there back to Black Hawk.

Each way was expensive and long. Once ore was hauled to Denver, it was just as easy to ship it east on the railroad. In 1868, the first assay of ore from the Dwight was shipped to Newark, New Jersey, according to Gardiner.

In 1873, a smelter was built at Dudley, near the foot of Mount Bross, and a Boston and Colorado Smelter was built in Alma.

Rich Ore

The highest yield of any carload of silver ore in Colorado came from the Moose Mine in the summer of 1872, according to a story first printed in the South Park–based *Mount Lincoln Sentinel* and reprinted in the *Denver Daily Times* on May 31, 1873.

That summer, eight men worked 120 days at the two-year-old Moose Mine. They produced 570 tons of ore and sorted it into three grades. The highest grade was shipped to Europe for smelting (use of heat to extract minerals from ore).

The shipment sent to Europe was worth $5,200 per ton, or in 2013 dollars, $102,000 per ton. During the silver boom, ore was considered unproductive if it contained two hundred ounces of silver or fewer per ton; ore containing four hundred ounces of silver per ton was very profitable.

The price of silver in 1872 was $1.325 per ounce. A ton of ore containing 200.0 ounces of silver was worth $265 in 1872, a ton containing 400.0 ounces was worth $530. To be worth $5,200 per ton, the 1872 European ore shipment contained 3,924.5 ounces of silver per ton.

And that silver ore was seemingly easy pickings. In the same story, the reporter from the *Sentinel* said he personally examined the Moose Mine and said the ore in the shipments was not mined. It "was taken simply from the drifts, shafts and cuts which were run to develop the mine" and "not one single pound of ore has been stoped [deliberately mined] out."

The reporter also said the ore yet to be mined was "a continuous vein of solid mineral 200 feet in length and from two to seven feet in width." Mining engineers of the day estimated the value of that vein at $2 million, the *Mount Lincoln Sentinel* said.

Only the very best specimens were sorted in the shipment bound for Europe; it was not a realistic sample of average ore value from the Moose. A more realistic estimate of the value of ore from the Moose is given in a story in the Pueblo-based *Colorado Daily Chieftain* of June 8, 1876. It said ore from the Moose assayed at between $150 and $600 per ton, and ore from the Dolly Varden typically assayed at $360 per ton. The Russia Mine on Mount Lincoln had the highest value of all in Park County, according to the *Chieftain*, at $700 per ton.

But the Mount Bross mines were no match when compared to Horace Tabor's Matchless Mine in Leadville, Colorado. According to www.matchlessmine.com, assays of that mine contained up to one thousand ounces of silver per ton of ore, or $1,325 per ton in 1872.

The mines on both sides of the Mosquito Range were making their owners rich, but then, silver values took a massive dive.

PANIC OF 1873

In 1873, Congress demonetized silver, meaning gold was then the only metal backing the nation's currency. Following that governmental decision, the country went into a depression.

But from reading Colorado newspapers of the day, one might not know of silver's devaluation. A story in the Georgetown-based *Daily Colorado Miner* of January 2, 1874, reported the Moose was mining a body of ore worth $400 per ton, with eighteen men working the mine.

The April 7, 1877 *Colorado Springs Gazette* reported that the Moose Mine was actively shipping ore each week to the Wyandotte Smelting and Refining Co. in Wyandotte, Michigan. That week, the Moose shipped 60,342 tons to Michigan, reportedly more than its average weekly load.

And Moose Mine owners were spending money on employee gifts. Mine superintendent Chas. Aill was reported to have received a $250 gold watch and chain on New Year's Day in the January 17, 1878 *Georgetown Courier*. That watch would be worth $5,800 in 2013.

To increase the price of silver, stocks were manipulated at the New York Stock Exchange "through newspaper stories about shipments of rich ore and rumors of valuable new strikes," said Gardiner's book.

A story in the June 27, 1877 Golden-based *Colorado Transcript* seems to verify Gardiner's statement: "Within ten days after the Moose mine was placed upon the New York stock boards, 19,000 shares were sold."

Despite what was reported (or not reported) in newspapers of the day, the economy was suffering. The government decided to take action to restore the bimetallism (silver and gold) base of the U.S. currency.

Partial Bimetallism

In 1878, silver was restored as legal tender, and the government started buying a minimal amount of silver each month; however, true bimetallism was not restored. No value was set on silver near the sixteen-to-one ratio in place between the years 1837 and 1873.

The change contributed to returned prosperity for the nation and to the Park County mines in the 1880s. The June 5, 1879 *Flume* was already reporting increased mining activity. The Dolly Varden was producing "splendid material," and the labor force was "larger than usual."

Also, it said, "The Russia [Mine] never looked so promising as at this time. There are newly opened courses of ore of the richest quality and in quantities that will last for years." The story reported that the new Russia discoveries alone had an estimated value of "nearly half a million."

And prosperity kept growing. The September 18, 1879 *Flume* reported 115 men working at the Moose Mine.

The *Leadville Democrat* of February 18, 1881, said, "The beginning of a new era is about to dawn [on Alma] if the present indications are anything to judge from." It said some important new strikes had been made, and the Moose Mine sent down "over $2,000 worth of ore last month."

The former Fairplay home of Assyria Hall, shown here in 2012, was built in 1876. *Author photo.*

Prosperity didn't last long. In 1887, hard times were back nationwide. It hit the mining industry in Alma even earlier.

The Dolly Varden was sold in February 1881 to the Boston Gold and Silver Mining Company, according to the *Leadville Daily Herald* of February 22, 1881, and the Moose was having problems by that summer.

"It is wrecked, but not exhausted," said *The Flume* of July 28, 1881, in a story about the Moose Mine. It said that the Dolly Varden was in worse shape three months previous and that it had pulled out and was "at the very head of Park County mines." *The Flume* was hopeful the Moose would pull out as well.

But silver mining was on a downward spiral. In February 1883, the Moose ownership was transferred in foreclosure to the Union Trust Company of New York, as reported by *The Flume* of February 8, 1883; the Alma smelter shut down in 1884, according to *The Flume* of January 24, 1884; and the mine dumps at the Moose and Dolly Varden were leased out, *The Flume* of July 5, 1888, recorded.

And then the government stepped in again.

SHERMAN SILVER PURCHASE ACT

In 1890, the Sherman Silver Purchase Act was instituted. It obligated the government to buy almost all the silver mined each month in the nation and to buy it at market rates. It also obligated the government to redeem notes in either gold or silver.

But as silver ore flooded the market, its price went down. Holders of government notes began to redeem notes for gold rather than silver, draining the nation's gold supply.

There were other factors, but the Sherman Act and its resultant gold drain may have contributed to the depression of 1893, according to www.u-s-history.com.

One result of the action was the continuous decline in silver value. In 1890, the price of an ounce of silver dipped to $1.16, according to the August 16, 1890 *Aspen Daily Chronicle*; the price dropped to $0.69 in December 1893, recorded the December 7, 1893 *Flume*; and it went to $0.60 in December 1894, said the December 13, 1894 *Flume*.

The Sherman Act was repealed in 1893, although that decision was debated in Congress until 1900. On November 1, 1895, U.S. mints stopped producing silver coins, and the New Orleans mint was closed. Silver dollars were shunned by banks, said the November 8, 1895 *Aspen Daily Times*.

Colorado senator Henry Teller said in August 1897 that he still believed in the need for silver backing of the treasury. He said that silver added more money to the economy. "The more money there is, the more industry there will be. There is not enough money as matters stand," he said in the August 13, 1897 *Flume*.

But after seven years of debate, the Gold Standard Act was passed in 1900. It established gold as the sole standard for U.S. currency.

In 1902, there was optimism that "gold mining, farming and fruit growing, the cattle industry, coal and iron production, manufacturing and other sources of wealth" would make the loss of silver values "less injurious as it would have been a few years ago," said the November 28, 1902 *Flume* in a reprint from the *Denver News*. The story concluded, "Yet it is a pity that adverse influences should be able to cripple the silver mining industry."

The price of silver in November 1902 was $0.48 per ounce. As of May 29, 2013, an ounce of silver was valued at $22.46, or about $0.83 cents in 1902.

1900s

Chapter 16

Pioneers Buried at Guffey

They Had Varied Occupations and Lifestyles; Early Lives Reveal History of Area

In the fall of 2012, a citizens' committee hired a firm to search for lost graves at the Guffey Cemetery. In using ground-penetrating radar, fifteen to twenty unknown and unmarked graves of early Guffey citizens were discovered. Before the radar work was begun, thirty-one sites were known.

These are the stories of a few Guffey pioneers who share a final resting place in the Guffey Cemetery. Their tales hint of the people who first settled in Guffey and the surrounding areas of Black Mountain and Current Creek at the turn of the twentieth century.

The cemetery is found on few maps, and a Google search won't get you there. You find it by walking down a narrow footpath through a ponderosa pine forest and up a hill to a majestic view.

But proceed with caution. In October 2012, officials were working to find the owner of the cemetery property. At that time, permission was granted by Park County sheriff Fred Wegener for me to tour the cemetery. Ownership was established in July 2013, but until an easement is established, there is no legal access to the site.

Early Guffey

It's hard to imagine when driving through Guffey today what the town was like when it was new. There were five hundred people living in town and

Guffey, Colorado, in an undated photo from its early years. *Park County Local History Archives, Sam and Bette Sciortino.*

another seven hundred in outlying areas. Gold miners first discovered the potential in the area in 1895; later, cattle and sheep ranchers sustained the town, and farmers had success growing potatoes. There were forty businesses within the town limits, rodeos were held on the street and the dance hall was a popular place for families; the dance hall also doubled as town hall. Businesses included mercantile and grocery stores, the Townsend Hotel and, after cars became popular, a filling station.

According to Helen Cahill in her book *Guffey: One Hundred Years of Memories*, the post office was first established on April 12, 1895, as Freshwater, named for the Freshwater Mining District. The name was later changed to Idaville in honor of local mine owner Ida McClavey Wagner. And on May 23, 1896, it was changed again, this time to Guffey, named for James M. Guffey of Pennsylvania.

Guffey was among the most successful individual producers of oil and natural gas in the United States, was instrumental in forming the Gulf Refining Company and was affiliated with Standard Oil. He was the committeeman representing Pennsylvania at the 1908 Democratic National Convention in Denver, but he was unseated at the convention because he did not support William Jennings Bryan as the presidential candidate.

According to Cahill's book, James Guffey may have had mining properties in the Freshwater district, and it is said he paid $500 to have the town named after him. In 2013, that $500 would be about $14,000.

James Guffey gave his name to the town, but it was the people moving into the area in the late 1890s and early 1900s that established the town of Guffey. Of those buried in the Guffey Cemetery, some were successful business owners, and others were ranchers who experienced bad luck. The children who died young and the old-timers who didn't all left their mark in this southeastern corner of Park County.

BABY BUFORD SWOPE

His full name may not have been "Baby" Buford, but that's the name on his headstone. He was a few days short of sixteen months old when he died on August 7, 1897, and is the youngest and probably the first person buried at Guffey. His parents were William and Marry Swope, who were originally from Missouri.

Baby Buford had an older brother and three older sisters: William, ten; Edna, seven; Edith, five; and Elsie, three. The elder William Swope ran several stores in town and is listed in the Colorado Business Directory for Guffey in 1901 (general merchandise) and 1905 (dry goods, boots and shoes). In 1907, it was reported in *The*

Grave of Baby Buford Swope at the Guffey Cemetery in 2012. *Author photo.*

Flume that a large copper strike was discovered on land William Swope coowned southwest of Guffey. He owned the first car in Guffey and, in 1908, was a Park County commissioner. By 1910, the family had moved to Cañon City.

W.T. BOUTWELL

According to a Boutwell family page on www.familytreemaker.com, William Thurston Boutwell died while visiting a friend in a Colorado mining town. He had been living in San Francisco for ten years before he arrived in Guffey in 1904 and was a widower for nine of those years. His first wife, Mary, died of pneumonia in 1895.

The friend Boutwell was visiting may have been Helen Curliss, who he married in Guffey at high noon on June 1, 1904, two months before his death. Curliss was a sister to Matilda Townsend, who ran the Townsend Hotel in Guffey. In its June 10, 1904 edition, *The Flume* wished the newlyweds "a long and happy life."

Boutwell is the only known Civil War soldier buried at Guffey and has the only military headstone there. He served in Company B, Thirteenth New Hampshire Infantry, from August 1862 to the war's end in 1865.

He was born on September 13, 1842, in New Hampshire and died on August 2, 1904, in Guffey at age sixty-one.

WILLIAM AND MATILDA TOWNSEND

William Townsend was a hotel proprietor when the 1900 census was taken on June 15 that year. It is a safe guess that his business was the Townsend Hotel, sometimes called the Townsend House. That was the name of the hotel his wife, Matilda Townsend, ran in Guffey after her husband's death.

He was born in New York on April 6, 1836, and died in Guffey on September 5, 1903. He was sixty-seven years old and has a marked grave at the Guffey Cemetery.

In her own obituary, Matilda Townsend was said to have "sterling qualities [and was] beloved by all." She also seems to have taken a no-nonsense approach to running the hotel.

PARKED IN THE PAST

In 1908, C.B. and Merle Dell were honeymooning at the Townsend Hotel. After the wedding, the couple's friends treated them to "an old-fashioned charivari" (discordant mock serenade to newlyweds), as reported in *The Flume* of June 19, 1908.

"Things were progressing nicely until Mrs. Townsend opened the door and threw a pan of water on Gus Cohen, which put a stop to all further proceedings," *The Flume* story said.

At the time, Matilda Townsend was a sixty-eight-year-old widow. Gus Cohen, fifty-one, owned "the largest pharmacy in town," according to advertisements of the day. In the Guffey portion of the 1910 *Colorado Business Directory*, Cohen's business enterprises were listed as "flour and feed, groceries, justice [of the] peace, postmaster." But Cohen's many accomplishments didn't stop the widow Townsend from controlling the noisy crowd at her hotel.

Matilda Townsend, originally from Michigan, died on August 10, 1909, at age sixty-nine and was buried next to her husband in the Guffey Cemetery.

WILLIAM FLAVIOUS "FLAVE" WHITE AND CHARITY KATE MCBETH WHITE

Flave and Kate White came to Guffey in 1896 from Macon County, Missouri, where they were married in September 1890; at the time, Flave was fifty-five and Kate was twenty-four. The 1900 U.S. census showed they lived in Cotopaxi, Colorado, in Fremont County with their four children—John, seven; Willetta, six; Virgil, five; and Alfred, two—but recollections by son Virgil as told in Cahill's book put the family in Guffey during the children's growing-up years. It is unknown but possible that after the parents died, relatives living in the area raised the children in Guffey.

There was a murder in Guffey soon after the family moved there. The town had no jail for the prisoner, so Flave White was appointed marshal and told to build a jail. He also helped build the dance hall, which doubled as the town hall. He was a farmer by trade.

According to *The Flume* of August 28, 1908, Flave White died on August 21, 1908, after an illness of many weeks. After a funeral at City Hall, he was buried at the Guffey Cemetery next to Kate White. She had died in 1903.

JOSEPH CARPENTER

On January 29, 1906, Joseph Carpenter was riding home when his horse spooked and started running; he fell off the horse and landed on his head. The injury was severe, and Carpenter died three days later on February 1. He is buried somewhere in the Guffey Cemetery.

Of French Canadian descent, Joseph Carpenter was forty-five years old in 1906 and living on the Roberts Ranch one mile outside of Guffey. He had lived there with his two daughters—Cora, eighteen, and Margaret, fourteen—for only a few weeks before the accident happened.

He was no stranger to the Guffey area, having lived there for ten years working as a miner. He had filed on two claims in the Freshwater Mining District and had recently taken up ranching to settle down "to a peaceable ranch life with his two daughters," *The Flume* of February 9, 1906, reported.

A peaceable life might not have been Carpenter's fate if he had lived. He filed for divorce in 1902 from his wife of fifteen years, Margaret Carpenter. He charged her with abandonment and desertion of him and their daughters and with "adultery…committed at various times…with [various] different men," the court summons read.

A story in the September 15, 1905 *Flume* indicated Margaret Carpenter caused more trouble to her husband than just her friendship with other men. She also spent time in the Fairplay jail in 1905 for theft from a Como store.

And the eldest daughter, Cora, may have picked up some of her mother's bad habits. *The Flume* said Cora "was inclined to be pretty [wild] and has been leading a merry life since her arrival at Guffey." She ran away from home earlier in 1905 and walked to Cañon City, a distance of thirty-three miles. She told authorities she was being abused by her father. She also said her father wanted her to marry a man she did not love.

Joseph Carpenter's story was that Cora was dating a bartender. Her father did not approve of the bartender and told Cora to stay away from him. She later went to a dance with the man and was scolded when she returned home.

In August 1905, Joseph Carpenter's ex-wife, Margaret Carpenter, and their daughter Cora allegedly stole a livery rig. They rented it in Cañon City and didn't return it. The owner of the rig had the two followed from Cañon City to Guffey and on to Victor. They were apprehended in Cripple Creek, and the rig was found in a Victor barn.

That edition of *The Flume* said no decision had been made on "what to do with the two women," and no further mention of the incident was found.

No record was found of the three Carpenter women after the January 1906 death of Joseph Carpenter. However, his estate was on the delinquent tax list through at least 1907.

Lawrence Walters

In 1906, Lawrence Walters was a rancher and miner, thirty-two years old and single. He lived with a brother, Goodie Walters, who was forty and also single. They worked the ranch and Black Mule Mine together. The brothers were of German descent and from Missouri.

It was reported in the April 20, 1906 *Flume* that on the afternoon of Easter Sunday, April 15, 1906, Lawrence Walters drove the seven miles into Guffey from his ranch in the Black Mountain area to pick up a spool of barbed wire. He carried a revolver in his holster.

When Lawrence Walters stooped to pick up the fence wire and put it in his wagon, the gun slipped out of his holster, struck the wire and discharged. A bullet hit Walters in his right lung, and he slowly bled to death. He died Sunday evening.

A sister, Lizzie Walters, arrived in Guffey the following Wednesday from St. Joseph, Missouri, *The Flume* edition of April 27 said, but she was too late to see her brother before he was buried at the Guffey Cemetery. The funeral and burial had taken place on Tuesday, April 17.

Walter Ballenger

Walter Ballenger has a headstone at the Guffey cemetery, but very little was discovered of his life. He was born in Spiceland, Indiana, on November 25, 1870, and died on January 31, 1902, at age thirty-one. The 1900 census listed his occupation as a harness maker. He lived in the Current Creek area of Fremont County.

Ballenger's grandparents Henry and Rebecca Ballenger were among the Quaker pioneers who founded Spiceland in the early 1800s. His parents, Nathan and Margaret Ballenger, were also prominent leaders in the Quaker Society of Friends in Spiceland. His father served in local politics.

Walter Ballenger had seven siblings and was from a long line of religious and political leaders. No indication was found of why he moved to Guffey.

Chapter 17

Maddox Ice Company

Employed Hundreds in Early 1900s,
Supplied Denver with Ice from Lakes Near Present–Day
Platte Canyon High School

In 2013, a football field and track occupied the land across U.S. 285 from the Bailey-based school complex, including Platte Canyon High School, Fitzsimmons Middle School and the Platte Canyon School District administration building between Bailey and Shawnee. But in the years from 1903 to 1937 at that site, the months of January and February were busy with another activity.

From two lakes in the area of the present-day athletic fields, the Maddox Ice Company shipped ice to Denver on the narrow-gauge Colorado & Southern Railroad. In the thirty-four-year span, the company seasonally employed one hundred or more men to cut and move huge blocks of ice from the frozen lakes onto railroad cars at the Maddox Depot.

The ice was shipped to 684 Alcott Street in Denver, where the Maddox family lived in a small house and stored the Platte Canyon ice in several warehouses on site.

When the ice arrived in Denver, another one hundred men were employed moving ice blocks from boxcars into warehouses. And throughout the year, but more often in summer, drivers delivered ice for use in residential and business iceboxes throughout Denver and its suburbs.

The logo of Maddox Ice Company taken from a plastic ice bag. *Author photo.*

MADDOX LAND PURCHASE

William Clay Maddox, called Clay when a given name was used at all in early issues of *The Flume*, came up the Platte Canyon from Denver in 1902 looking for acreage to build lakes for an ice business. He found what he was looking for on 320 acres of pastureland between Bailey and Shawnee.

Although the name of Shawnee had been used only since 1900, a settlement had been at that location since 1878, and it was first called

Fairville and, later, Slaghts. The 320 acres Maddox bought excluded the 8 acres that composed the town of Shawnee.

Maddox and the seller, Alfred Crebbin, closed the deal on January 1, 1903, for $3,500 cash. In 2013, the amount would be close to $92,000—not a bad deal for 320 acres with water rights—but quite a bit of cash to carry from Denver on the train.

Maddox named his business H.J. Maddox & Company; the H.J. was in honor of his wife, Hilda Josephine. Later, the name was changed to Maddox Ice Company.

ICE HARVEST

The Maddox Ice Company built two lakes on the property. They were drained long ago, but there is a lake in the vicinity today that covers a portion of the former Maddox property.

Arthur Hall, past president of the Park County Historical Society and a longtime resident of the area, said the upper Maddox Lake "did cover most of the area where the current lake is."

When the weather got cold enough for two feet of ice to form on the lakes, the Maddox community was alive with the sounds of horses pulling scrapers across the frozen lakes to remove snow. Once that was done, workers would guide the horses in lines as straight as possible to score the ice, followed by men using gasoline-powered saws to cut blocks in uniform widths.

Each block was cut to the same size. The bottoms of the blocks, those that were on the underside of the lake, had to be trimmed and scraped because that side was never even. When that work was done, conveyor belts moved the ice blocks to train boxcars where they would be packed in insulating sawdust for shipment to Denver.

In an average winter, the company was able to harvest two cuttings of ice blocks, usually during the months of January and February.

SHIPMENT TO DENVER

Brownie Anderson, Como-based railroad engineer with the Colorado & Southern, operated the ice trains when Maddox was in business. He called the harvest the "January ice rush," according to a September 29, 2005 interview recorded with his son, Andy Anderson, found on the Park County Local History Archives website, www.parkcoarchives.org.

"And of course they used every boxcar they could find," said Andy Anderson.

> *And they had to work around the clock. They'd load twenty cars of ice, big blocks about the size of that sofa. They had big power saws out there sawing them up; they'd load them there in sawdust, and they'd make another move and load another boxcar [and] another boxcar and soon as that one was loaded, they headed toward Denver. Of course, in those days all of Denver was supplied by ice; they had iceboxes. They had the old ice truck and the guy with the tongs and the leather jacket on. He had to go up two flights of stairs with thirty, forty pounds of ice.*

In his book *Bits and Pieces of History Along the 285 Corridor*, the late Park County historian Harold Warren said that in one shipment in January 1905, Maddox Ice Company sent thirty trainloads of twenty cars each, or six hundred loads of ice, to its warehouses in Denver. And they couldn't ship all they had cut. Ice filled two warehouses near the lakes, ready for another shipment.

Earl Maddox, son of the founder, was quoted in a February 27, 1977 *Denver Post* story as saying, "There would be days we'd pull 80 train carloads of ice out of those lakes. We'd bring the ice to Denver to store it, in sawdust, for the season's use."

SIZE OF BLOCKS

One may wonder about the size of a block of ice. Anderson, quoted above, said that each was as big as a sofa.

The caption of a grainy photo on the Park County Local History Archives website showing a man maneuvering a block of ice up an incline on a conveyor belt reads, "Each ice block weighed about 1,800 [pounds]." In the photo, the block appears to be six or seven feet long and two feet thick.

For customers, the blocks were cut into smaller portions to fit each icebox; those portions cost the customer between fifteen and thirty cents each.

Warren's wife, the late Lenore Warren, lived in Denver as a child. She was quoted in the March 23, 1983 *South Park Times* in a story called "Bailey's

Early day ice delivery by Maddox in Englewood, Colorado. *Photo courtesy of the Englewood (Colorado) Public Library.*

Frozen Past" as saying, "It seems to me my mother would get 25 cents' worth to fill our little icebox."

She said Maddox was "the big ice company in Denver," and every child admired the man who delivered ice. At each stop the iceman made, he would chip the block of ice to get it exactly the right size for the order. She said the children would hang around the ice truck to pick up the cold slivers of ice—they were a special treat on a hot summer day.

Setbacks

Life wasn't always good for Maddox Ice. The February 22, 1907 *Flume* reported, "Mr. Maddox and ice crew went to Denver Sunday," meaning they left before the ice season was over.

The story continued, "It is feared the houses at Maddox will not be filled, as the ice is melting rapidly."

February was warm that year, as evidenced by two sentences in the same February 22 edition, saying, "Summer weather still continues" and "How is this for a Florida climate?"

And then there were employee problems. The February 14, 1908 *Flume* reported on the trial of "three rowdies, employed by the Maddox Ice company [*sic*], who created so much disturbance during the ice cutting at Maddox."

They were accused of playing pranks on fellow employees that "were nothing less than brutality to the extent of bodily injury."

The Flume doesn't tell exactly what happened; it just says that a Maddox employee "suffered bruises as the result of penalties imposed upon him by their kangaroo court." The rowdies were each fined three dollars and costs and were lectured by the court.

RECREATIONAL USE

Maddox knew the frozen lakes would be a draw for people living in Bailey and Shawnee, and he freely allowed ice-skating, with one stipulation. *The Flume* of January 29, 1904, said, "Mr. Maddox wishes it understood that fires on or about the lake are strictly prohibited."

In the summer, it was a different story. To keep the ice pure, he put up signs saying, "Keep out, absolutely no fishing, hunting or loafing." He did not want anyone near the lakes when they were not frozen.

PURE, CLEAN WATER

Maddox's rules kept the water and ice pure. The Denver-based Von Schulz and Low Chemical Laboratory tested the ice from the Maddox lakes. The report, as quoted in the *South Park Times* story, said, "The water, and therefore the ice from which it was derived, [is] remarkable for its extreme purity." And, it said, "It is purer even than many rain waters. We believe it to be the purest natural water, including artesian water, of which we have any record."

Men were working on the Maddox lakes even before the water froze, to ensure the ice would be pure. A mention in the November 25, 1904 *Flume* said that "a crew of 18 men are cleaning and floating the leaves and rubbish out of the Maddox ice in preparation for the coming cold weather."

The local newspaper acknowledged the quality of the ice on the Maddox lakes and reported it to the public. A December 8, 1905 *Flume* story said, "The best of ice is now freezing on the Maddox lake [*sic*]. The lake has been floated several times to clear away all the dust, leaves and other rubbish."

Given the heavy traffic on U.S. 285 and the increased population since 1937, it is unlikely a water test would show that amount of purity today.

THE END

Two events occurred in the late 1930s that curtailed the lucrative ice business in Platte Canyon for Maddox and its competitors. The Colorado & Southern narrow-gauge railroad shut down in 1937, taking away the means to economically move the ice to Denver. And in 1938, electric refrigerators were replacing iceboxes as the standard for storing food.

After the train route shut down, Maddox bought ice from other plants in Denver and continued a gradually reduced home delivery service. It saw a small boom in deliveries during World War II when "people couldn't buy new electrics during the war, or even get some of the old ones fixed," said Earl Maddox in the *Denver Post* story. But by 1950, home delivery of ice had stopped.

Maddox Ice continued to operate as late as 1983, packaging ice for retail sales, but no evidence could be found that the company is in business today.

The land previously occupied by Maddox Ice Company at 684 Alcott Street in Denver in 2013 is in use by Robinson Dairy.

1940s

Chapter 18

COMO HIGH SCHOOL

An Unplanned Time Capsule of Earlier Days, Artifacts
Uncovered from Como's Heyday

At a Park County board of county commissioner's meeting in July 2011, a time capsule was opened from the former McNamara Hospital building, completed in 1966. It contained photographs, postcards, a poster for the 1965 Burro Days celebration and a *Denver Post* story about limited funding for the new hospital. The items were purposely chosen as representative of life in Fairplay at the time.

But imagine how much more history would be revealed if items weren't chosen with particular care. Consider how much our descendants would learn about each of us if, in the instant this sentence is read, our homes were locked and all our possessions were untouched for seventy years.

It happened at the Como High School. An entire building—an unplanned time capsule—has been preserved since the early 1940s.

That's when the high school closed and busing to Fairplay began. It was locked with all of the school's supplies, books and science experiments inside. A few years later, the larger grade school closed, and when that building was remodeled into a community hall, elementary school memorabilia was moved into the high school for storage.

And the school sat, barely touched, until sometime in the 1990s.

Some hidden treasures of the past are just now being discovered, as the community comes together in its effort to record and preserve the past.

Como school in the 1890s before there was a separate high school. *Park County Local History Archives, Boot-Hall Family Collection.*

Students in front of the Como grade school in 1936. *From left*: William White, Mary Ethel James, Marion Gibbony, Hugh White, Stanley Nelson and Keith Schnurbusch. *Park County Local History Archives.*

1940

By 1940, trains no longer ran from Como to link it with Denver, Breckenridge, Leadville and Gunnison. The last train left the station in April 1937, and the tracks were pulled up in 1938. The automobile route over Boreas Pass was constructed in the 1950s, but in 1940, Como was dying a slow death.

Only one student, Marion Gibbony, graduated in 1940. Gibbony's cousin and Como native Gertrude Anderson (Como High School class of 1936) said in a June 2011 conversation with me in the old Como grade school that the last class to graduate from Como High School was her cousin's class.

It could be that the school went on for one year longer; there is a partial draft of a high school annual in the old school for the term of 1940–41 and a newsletter written by students dated March 1941. It could be there were no seniors in 1941.

EARLY SCHOOL HISTORY

In 1882, the South Park Line was completed to Breckenridge, and soon, up to twenty-six trains a day passed through Como. Families of railroaders moved to Como, and in 1883, a large school was built on the hill above town at Sixth and Spruce Streets.

Como was in its prime in 1910. It was the largest town in Park County, with a population of 475, according to the 1910 U.S. census. There were eighty-three school-age children (ages six to seventeen).

The next largest town was Alma, at 401 residents, followed by Fairplay, with 311. There was no listing for Bailey in the 1910 census, but Chase, near present-day Shawnee, had 119 residents, and 210 people were counted at Deer Valley, near the present-day Bailey-based Horn Cemetery.

As Como grew, the town realized the need for a separate high school. In 1930, an abandoned Presbyterian church was moved to a site near the original school, and it became Como High School.

And inside that converted church was discovered a historian's dream, a hodgepodge of classroom memorabilia with discoveries (so far) dating from about 1910 into the 1940s.

TIMEWORN TREASURES

The mementos left in the high school are not valuable in a monetary sense, but they give a glimpse into the history of the Como schools and of the students and teachers who made their mark in Como. Student surnames recorded in teachers' registers are names prominent in the railroading era; some of those students became second-generation railroaders.

Seeing the school is a rare treat. It is open to the public each year on Boreas Pass Railroad Day, and fortunate students of varying ages and backgrounds visit the historic structure on field trips. During those trips, they experience a day of school taught as it was decades ago.

Interior of Como High School in September 2012. *Author photo.*

School Memorabilia

One wonders what catches the attention of modern-day students.

It might be the large jar with the rusted lid that smells strongly of formaldehyde. The jar no longer contains the preserving liquid, but it does contain two crawdads that probably look much the same as they did when unknown schoolchildren placed them in the jar more than seventy years ago.

Or it could be the classroom-sized *Dick and Jane* book. The pages flip up in a design made so it can be placed in the front of the room so all young students can read together: "Dick. See Dick. See Dick run."

Classroom-sized *Dick and Jane* reader in the Como High School in 2012. *Author photo.*

Maybe children have an eye on the teacher's paddle, kept handy in earlier days to discipline unruly students. Some time ago, the paddle was used to stir a can of paint, and it now carries that stain.

TEACHER REGISTERS

It's not a full collection, but teachers' registers from several years are among the items at the school. From those books, history scholars have a list of students for the term, with boys' and girls' names on separate pages.

From one register that looks almost new, we know that on Tuesday, September 3, 1912, school started in Como. Esther S. Martin made ninety dollars per month teaching between nine and nineteen students each term (nineteen in the fall term, nine in the winter term and thirteen in the spring term) in grades one through eight. We know what textbooks were used and who visited the school.

It is interesting that Martin was the only teacher who wrote that the condition of the school was "bad, very bad." Teachers in other years recorded the school condition as "medium."

Martin wrote in her remarks, "The school house needs a thorough cleaning. It should have a new floor. The whole building needs to be carefully fumigated."

She also said the school needed some good wall maps and "new [window] shades are almost a necessity—for the good of the pupils' eyes."

Martin taught in the 1913–14 term as well. And in that year's teacher register, she was still requesting a new floor, maps and window shades. In addition to a rope for the school flag, she requested "a damper in the stove pipe to save fuel on windy days." She also requested "two screens, one for each window, to keep out the flies which torment the children for months."

CLASSES

A wide variety of textbooks were found in the old school. And from those, we know children raised in Como received a well-rounded education. High school classes from Donald O. Durning's 1935 teacher register included physics, English, algebra, economics, sociology, world progress history, biology and typing. We know that at one time, Latin and French languages and commercial law were taught; well-worn textbooks in those subjects were found in the school.

Incidentally, Durning was not only the teacher but also the principal. He was a college graduate with Bachelor of Arts and Bachelor of Education degrees and had thirty-six months of teaching experience. He made $125 per month and was the only teacher in the high school. There were twenty-two students in grades nine through twelve. His salary equals about $2,100 per month in 2013.

BOOKS

Mark Twain once said, "The man who does not read books has no advantage over the man that cannot read them."

If students in Como did not read, it was not due to lack of books. Numerous boxes of books were stored in the Como High School for more than seventy years. The books have been catalogued and may soon be available for use again. The Como Civic Association, owner of the two historic schools, has plans to allow book use inside the old grade school.

There are several collections of textbooks on many subjects for elementary through high school students. And there are single copies of other books.

One example is a rain-damaged but still legible edition of the *Complete Story of the San Francisco Horror* about the earthquake of 1906. It includes graphic photos of the destruction experienced in California, including photos of thieves robbing the dead and dying.

There is *Franklin: His Life by Himself*, published in 1891. The book includes a photo of Benjamin Franklin, looking much younger than on the current U.S. $100 bill, but with the same hairstyle and physique.

One book, *Lessons in English, Book Two* by Arthur Lee, gave the students knowledge of sentence structure and relationships between verbs, nouns, adverbs and adjectives.

The Presidents of the United States is a book about the lives of the presidents "from Washington to the present time." It ends with Benjamin Harrison, who was the twenty-third president and left office in 1893.

Chapter 19

FAIRPLAY'S HEALTHCARE HISTORY

In 1966, McNamara Was Modern Replacement for
Old County Hospital; A Look Back into Fairplay's
Healthcare History

The condemned, asbestos-ridden McNamara Building in Fairplay was torn down in 2012, and two Park County services buildings now stand in that location, one housing Emergency Services and the other housing Public Health, Human Services and Victim Services.

But for many years, the McNamara Hospital was a vital part of the community.

When the McNamara Building was completed in August 1966, it was the McNamara Hospital, named for Dr. Bradley Edward McNamara, or Dr. Mac, as he was known throughout the county.

The hospital was the modern replacement to former Fairplay Hospital at 550 Castello Avenue, built in the late 1800s as a home and, in 2013, used as an apartment building.

McNAMARA CONSTRUCTION

The McNamara Hospital was built for $257,289 in 1966. Comparing that to the cost to demolish the aged McNamara Building—$343,130 as reported in the November 11, 2011 *Flume*—it appears at first glance that the cost to tear down the building is nearly $100,000 more than what was paid to build it.

But that is before adjusting for inflation. In 2013, the construction cost of the McNamara Hospital was equivalent to about $1.85 million. And comparing 2013 to 1966, the cost to tear it down is equal to about $49,000.

The former McNamara Hospital in November 2011, shortly before it was torn down. *Author photo.*

In 1966, the county was pinching pennies. The hospital was built at about three-fourths of the typical cost for a small hospital at the time. The Denver-based architect Robert G. Irwin drew the plans "stripped of all frills," he said in an *Empire* magazine article of November 1, 1964.

Of the original cost, $151,117 came from Hill-Burton funds, a grant and loan program in place from 1946 to 1997 that provided money for hospitals to be built or modernized. The hospitals, in return, agreed to provide a reasonable volume of services to persons unable to pay and to use at least 51 percent of the building area in direct medical care to patients.

DR. MCNAMARA

McNamara, "a tall, broad-shouldered, ruddy-faced" forty-six-year-old, according to the *Empire* article, who specialized in emergency surgery, moved from Michigan with his wife, Jean, and four of their five children in 1962. They moved for the same reason many current residents do. "Because we like it here," McNamara said in the *Empire* article.

Marie Chisholm, a Park County resident since 1944 and a wealth of information on its history, remembers McNamara as a calm man, "a good doctor who never got rattled" when emergencies happened.

McNamara was an army doctor during World War II, leaving the service with the rank of major. He served as the county coroner and was a member of the original county planning commission.

For ten years beginning in 1962, McNamara had offices in both Fairplay and Bailey, using the most modern medical equipment available. He spent three afternoons a week in Bailey and the rest of his working time at the Fairplay hospital.

The Bailey clinic closed in 1972 when McNamara could no longer commute because he was recovering from major surgery. He died a year later, in August 1973, in the emergency room of his namesake hospital. But he didn't die as a patient. He had just finished saving his second emergency case of the day on August 26, when he suffered a fatal heart attack at age fifty-seven.

McNamara Hospital Money Woes

Both the McNamara Hospital and the hospital it replaced were opened to treat emergencies, obstetrics, minor surgery and critical major surgery where travel could be life threatening, as well as to serve as nursing homes.

The financial condition of Fairplay's older hospital could not be found, but the McNamara Hospital had money problems almost from the day it opened.

Within three years of opening, the new McNamara Hospital was in the red. In 1969, it was in debt by $46,000, and by 1973, the debt was $65,000, according to a letter dated October 10, 1972, to then Governor John A. Love from Roy Cleere, M.D., the then state director of public health. Adjusting for inflation as of 2013, the figures seem substantially higher, $293,000 in 1969 and by 1973, $342,000. The letter asked for "financial relief from the Governor's Emergency Fund."

An article in the October 30, 1992 *Flume*, recapping the history of McNamara Hospital, tells of efforts to recoup losses. Mercy Hospital leased McNamara, and it became known as McNamara-Mercy in 1974. The county commissioners took back control in about August 1980, but it was leased out again, this time to Porter Hospital, in September 1981 until November 21, 1984, when the hospital closed for good.

After the hospital closed, the building was used in succession as the South Park Clinic, the Silverheels Clinic under the auspices of Park County Rural Health and as various county offices. It was condemned and vacated in 2009.

OLD FAIRPLAY HOSPITALS

An older, eight-bed Park County Hospital in Fairplay existed as early as 1892, but the building at 550 Castello Avenue was the first Fairplay hospital of the twentieth century. It was built as a home in either 1875 or 1899 (sources differ on the year). It was later converted to a boardinghouse and, at one time, was headquarters for the local Ku Klux Klan, according to the *Empire* article.

It was converted to the Fairplay Hospital in 1929 and was used for that purpose until January 1965, when it was condemned as a firetrap. The building is used in 2013 as an apartment building.

As a sixteen-year-old Fairplay High School student in the winter of 1946–47, Chisholm was a nurse's aide on the night shift at the Castello Avenue hospital. She was hired to make beds, give baths and serve meals to the patients.

But her duties turned out to be more than that. Many times, Chisholm was the only staff member on the floor. When an emergency came in, Chisholm would admit the patient and inform whichever doctor or nurse was on call. They would give her instructions and get to the hospital as soon as they could.

A 1965 view of the old Fairplay Hospital at 550 Castello Street. In 2013, it is an apartment building. *Park County Local History Archives, South Park Historical Society.*

In 1965, patients at the old Fairplay Hospital had to climb the stairs for surgery or childbirth. *Park County Local History Archives, South Park Historical Society.*

Sometimes, the care from Chisholm, only a teenager, was all the care a patient received for hours.

Chisholm was working alone one night when a woman who was seven months pregnant came into the hospital. She had been helping fight a fire that had broken out in her home, and the activity had brought on labor pains. The doctor on call was in Boulder, at least a three- or four-hour drive on the then two-lane U.S. 285. The woman was able to walk up the narrow stairway to the delivery/operating room but nearly bled to death from complications of the pregnancy. The doctor made it back in time, and mother and baby survived.

"I don't know how he got there so fast," said Chisholm. But she was glad he did. The family still visits Fairplay; they own a second home on Front Street.

Another of her duties was assisting during surgeries.

One time, she was working the suction machine during a child's tonsillectomy. The child bled a lot, and the suction machine got full. She yelled to the cook in the kitchen to bring a large pan. The cook brought the pan, and Chisholm emptied the suction machine. The cook just about fainted—she was holding the pan.

There was an area of the hospital that was called "the back porch," Chisholm said. This area was used as a nursing home where indigents and those on old-age pensions lived out their lives. But it wasn't called a nursing home; it was just called "the back porch" and was an addition with lots of windows around it, like a covered porch. On slow nights, Chisholm was able to get a few hours of sleep as long as she woke up when the back porch residents needed her.

Another high school girl from Fairplay worked when Chisholm was off duty. Chisholm said that one time when the other girl was on duty, a man was brought in who had nearly cut off his leg in a ranching accident. The leg couldn't be saved, and the decision was made to amputate. The high school girl assisted with the surgery by holding the man's leg. She later told Chisholm: "It sure felt strange to have that leg come off in my hands."

Chisholm helped with surgeries frequently, but she said she never delivered a baby, except, she said, her own. Her first child, Keith, was born at the old Fairplay Hospital in 1955.

1950s

Chapter 20

SUMMER 1954

Camp Carson Soldiers March Through County;
"The Looters" Filmed in Eleven Mile Canyon;
Sixth Annual Burro Days

The route from Fairplay, Colorado, to Colorado Springs along Colorado Highway 9 and U.S. 24 is a quick, smooth motor vehicle ride on a modern highway.

That mileage was more of a challenge when, in late June 1954, Camp Carson (now Fort Carson) soldiers from the Eighth Infantry reversed the route, going from the army base south of Colorado Springs to the highest elevations of Park County on their way to Camp Hale near Leadville—and they did it on foot.

Contributing to the exhausting trek was the weather. At about the time the marchers were leaving Camp Carson, the Colorado Springs area was in the midst of a heat wave, with one-hundred-degree record temperatures reached on June 23 and 24. As of June 2012, the records for those days have not been broken.

The soldiers left Camp Carson and traveled, whenever possible, on forest service roads through the Pike National Forest. They passed through Manitou Springs, Woodland Park, Divide, Lake George, Hartsel, Garo and Fairplay before marching over Mosquito Pass to arrive at Camp Hale, twenty miles west of Leadville in Eagle County.

The group was at Camp Hale for training in July and August. The training lasted a little over a month. They learned mountain maneuvers such as rock climbing, mountain climbing, mountain evacuations for injured personnel and nighttime mountain deployment.

The September 3, 1954 *Flume* reprinted an article from the *Colorado Springs Gazette Telegraph* that said, in reporting the return of another regiment—

Private First Class Thomas F. Weirich (left) and Private First Class Robert W. O'Brien in July 1954 at Camp Hale, Colorado, twenty miles west of Leadville. *Photo courtesy of Thomas Weirich.*

the Thirteenth Infantry—to Carson from Hale, "Nearly 10,000 men from Carson have undergone the summer phase of mountaineering at the two-mile-high post, the largest training program to be held there since World War II."

SOLDIERS

Private First Class Thomas F. Weirich, assigned to Medical Company, Sixty-first Infantry Regiment, Eighth Infantry Division, at Camp Carson was one of the soldiers who didn't march from the army base.

He drove a three-quarter-ton, four-by-four truck loaded with medical and personal supplies for the soldiers riding in the truck to the summit of Mosquito Pass. The mission was to set up a medical aid station that was used for three days, from June 28 to 30, "to provide medical support to infantry soldiers and their attached company medics who marched over 'The Pass' on their way to Camp Hale, Colorado," said Weirich.

Weirich said the soldiers needed only minor medical attention at the Mosquito Pass summit. "A few needed a whiff of oxygen, some needed minor care for foot problems, and some needed cough medicine (the famous G.I. gin)."

G.I. gin was a cough syrup, heavy in codeine and alcohol, that could stop just about any cough immediately.

MOSQUITO PASS

Weirich had never driven a road like Mosquito Pass. But he was successful.

After another army vehicle bogged down in mud and snowmelt in a meadow below the summit and its driver gave up driving the pass, Weirich picked up the two medics and the regimental surgeon from that vehicle. They joined him and his medic passenger to continue en route to the top. The surgeon rode with Weirich in the cab, and the three medics rode on the tailgate and walked at times when the going got rough.

The road was evidently in no better shape in 1954 than it is today.

Weirich took the canvas cover off the back of the truck and folded down the windshield for better visibility. Even so, at one point, Weirich said in a telephone conversation, "I looked out—all I could see was space."

One time along the route, the truck stopped working due to the altitude and the heat of the engine, "a case of vapor lock," Weirich said in an e-mail. To fix the problem, he cut an orange in half and hollowed it out. He filled it with snow and placed the orange on top of the fuel pump. Weirich said that in about ten minutes, he was able to start the truck again and proceed up the pass.

On one hairpin turn in the road, Weirich had to back up and ease forward three times to get the army vehicle around the bend. But he made it. He said of his experience driving Mosquito Pass: "It was in the days [when] we had the courage of ignorance."

Private First Class Thomas F. Weirich (right) stands with an unknown medic on June 28, 1954, shortly before he drove the army truck to the top of Mosquito Pass. *Photo courtesy of Thomas Weirich.*

MOVIE MAKING

While the soldiers were training at Camp Hale, the movie *The Looters* was in production at Eleven Mile Canon.

The film, starring Julia Adams and Rory Calhoun, began filming in August for a May 1955 release date. According to the August 19, 1954 *Flume*, half of the movie was filmed there. Parts of the film were also shot on Park County's Tarryall Creek.

It told the story of a "plane crash in the rugged Rocky Mountains." The poster advertised, "Five desperate men...and a girl who didn't care... trapped on a mountain of gale-lashed rock!"

Adams, age eighty-five in June 2012, was then a young beauty in the beginning of her career. She acted in fifty-nine movies, beginning in 1949's *Red, Hot and Blue* and ending in a bit part in the 2011 release *Chez Upshaw*. Her credits include more than one hundred television appearances, most notably ten episodes of *Murder, She Wrote*.

The handsome male lead was played by Rory Calhoun, who died in 1999 at the age of seventy-six. His acting career began after he was paroled from San Quentin State Prison in California shortly before his twenty-first birthday. He was discovered while riding a horse in the Hollywood Hills, where he met actor Alan Ladd, whose wife was an agent. He starred in around seventy-two movies, beginning with *Something for the Boys* in 1944 and leading to *Pure Country* in 1992. He was a guest star in several television westerns—including *Bonanza*, *Wagon Train* and *Gunsmoke*—and he appeared in *The Blue and Gray* miniseries in 1982.

Burro Days

The sixth annual Burro Days celebration and its burro race from Leadville to Fairplay was predicted to be the "best ever" in the July 15, 1954 *Flume*. Starr Yelland—radio personality at Denver stations KOA and KLZ, then a member of the South Park Chamber of Commerce and, since 2001, an inductee into the Broadcast Professionals Hall of Fame—was master of ceremonies of the burro race that year.

The parade featured a forty-five-piece marching band from Cripple Creek, Colorado; a "glass wagon" float from State Game & Fish; and a "nationally publicized float" by Coors Brewing, courtesy of the Fairplay Distributing Company. Prizes for parade floats totaled $175.

It was reported in the August 5 *Flume* that Leadville's Tim Martin was first over the finish line, with a time of 4 hours, 17 minutes and 42.5 seconds. He gave his burro, Red, a big kiss after they won the race.

Eve Perkins, an "attractive Leadville teacher," was the third woman over the line. The attractiveness of other racers was not reported.

Prize money has not changed as much as one might expect since the sixth annual race. The first-place prize was $700 ($1,000 in 2011), second place was $400 ($800 in 2011) and third place was $300 ($500 in 2011). In addition, there was a fourth-place prize of $100 awarded in 1954.

For guessing the winning time of the first-place finisher, the 2011 prize was $500. But in 1954, guessing the winning time paid off better than winning the race. The person who guessed the winning time was awarded $1,000. There were also prizes for being second and third in guessing the winning time.

MONTGOMERY DAM

The July 15, 1954 *Flume* reported that a bid had been accepted by Fisher Contracting of Phoenix to build a dam to flood the former town site of Montgomery, north of Alma. It was to hold five thousand acre-feet of municipal water for the city of Colorado Springs. The bid was $2,247,672, which was below the engineers' estimate of $3,000,000.

STABBING

There was at least one instance of a soldier bringing his wife to the Camp Hale area, where the couple was housed in a temporary home, that may have caused stress in the marriage.

The July 15, 1954 *Flume* reported that Sergeant First Class Duane A. Livengood of Oregon was fatally stabbed by his wife, Francis A. Livengood, at their temporary home five miles east of Leadville near Camp Hale. It was reported that they were "fighting and arguing all evening." She was taken to the Lake County jail.

CHANGING TIMES

Phone numbers were easier to remember back then. *The Flume* number was 29.

A new Ford F-100 pickup cost $1,695 (state and local taxes extra).

The Fairplay Hospital reported patient names each week, including why the person was admitted, when the person was released and whether the person died while in the hospital. The report included who had tonsillectomies and what town they lived in, which staff members were on vacation and who replaced vacationing staffers.

AAA advised tourists to avoid cities during rush hours to "save time and prevent strained nerves," as reported in the August 5, 1954 *Flume*.

The state of Colorado was expecting four million visitors in 1954, according to the July 15, 1954 *Flume*. By comparison, in 2011, the Colorado Tourism Office reported the record was broken for number of visitors to the state, at 57.9 million.

BIBLIOGRAPHY

BOOKS

Amitrani, E.J. "Gene." *A Town Is Born: The Story of South Park City.* Fairplay, CO: self-published, 1982.

Andrew, Chris O. *The Legend of Benjamin Ratcliff.* Gainesville, FL: Bookends Press, 2011.

Bancroft, Caroline. *Augusta Tabor: Her Side of the Scandal.* Boulder, CO: Johnson Publishing Company, 1972.

———. *Silver Queen: The Fabulous Story of Baby Doe Tabor.* Boulder, CO: Johnson Publishing Company, 1989.

Barth, Richard. *Pioneers of the Colorado Parks.* Caldwell, ID: Claxton Printers Ltd., 1997.

Blevins, Tim, Dennis Daily, Chris Nicholl, Calvin P. Otto and Katherine Scott Sturdevant. *Extraordinary Women of the Rocky Mountain West.* Colorado Springs, CO: Pikes Peak Library District, 2010.

Bowen, A.W. & Company. *Progressive Men of Western Colorado.* Chicago: A.W. Bowen & Company, 1905.

Cahill, Helen. *Guffey: One Hundred Years of Memories.* Guffey, CO: Guffey Community Association, 1995.

Chapman Publishing Company. *Portrait and Biographical Record of Denver and Vicinity Colorado.* Chicago: Chapman Publishing Company, 1898.

———. *Portrait and Biographical Record of the State of Colorado.* Chicago: Chapman Publishing Company, 1899.

Coel, Margaret, and Sam Speas. *Goin' Railroading.* Boulder, CO: Pruett Publishing Company, 1985.

Cook, David J. *Hands Up; or, Thirty-Five Years of Detective Life in the Mountains and on the Plains: A Condensed Criminal History of the Far West.* Denver, CO: W.F. Robinson Printing Company, 1897.

Dyer, J.L. *The Snow-Shoe Itinerant: An Autobiography of Rev. John L. Dyer.* Cincinnati, OH: Cranston & Stowe, 1889.

Epperson, Harry A. *Colorado As I Saw It.* Kaysville, UT: Inland Printing Company, 1944.

Fossett, Frank. *Colorado: Its Gold and Silver Mines, Farms and Stock Ranges and Health and Pleasure Resorts: Tourist's Guide to the Rocky Mountains.* New York: C.G. Crawford, Printer and Stationer, 1880.

Gardiner, Harvey N. *Mining Among the Clouds.* Denver: Colorado Historical Society, 2002.

Howbert, Irving. *Memories of a Lifetime in the Pikes Peak Region.* New York: G.P. Putnam's Sons, 1925.

Mayer, Frank H., and Charles B. Roth. *The Buffalo Harvest.* Union City, TN: Pioneer Press, 1995.

McGrath, Maria Davies. *The Real Pioneers of Colorado.* Denver, CO: Denver Museum, 1934.

Smith, Duane A. *Horace Tabor, His Life and the Legend.* Niwot: University Press of Colorado, 1989.

Stewart, Robert Laird. *Sheldon Jackson, Pathfinder and Prospector of the Missionary Vanguard in the Rocky Mountains and Alaska.* New York: Fleming H. Revell Company, 1908.

Stone, Wilbur Fiske. *History of Colorado.* Vol. 4. Chicago: S.J. Clarke Publishing Company, 1919.

Warren, Harold. *Bits and Pieces of History Along the 285 Corridor: From Denver to Kenosha Pass.* Bailey, CO: K.R. Systems Inc., 1994.

DOCUMENTS

District court records. Levi Streeter, Anna Speas, Lillian Kennedy trial. Park County Courthouse, Fairplay, CO.

District court trial transcripts. Benjamin Ratcliff trial. Park County Local History Archives, Bailey, CO.

Guiraud File. Park County Local History Archives, Bailey, CO.

Websites

Adams, Julie, Biography. www.julieadams.biz/bio/bio.html.

Calhoun, Rory, Biography. www.imdb.com/name/nm0001983/bio.

Calhoun, Rory, Filmography. www.imdb.com/name/nm0001983.

Colorado Tourism Office. Record-Breaking Tourism Growth in 2011. www.colorado.com.

findagrave.com.

Greenback Movement. http://www.britannica.com.

Hill-Burton Free and Reduced-Cost Health Care. http://www.hrsa.gov/gethealthcare/affordable/hillburton.

Jim Reynolds, Confederate Guerilla. http://adamjamesjones.wordpress.com.

Moonshiners, Robbers and Frontier Law. http://historicjeffco.wordpress.com.

National Weather Service Forecast Office, Pueblo, Colorado. Dog Days of Summer. www.crh.noaa.gov/pub/events/heat2003.php.

Reynolds Gang Buried Treasure. http://www.legendsofamerica.com.

Reynolds Gang Stolen Treasure. http://learngoldprospecting.com.

The Looters Movie Poster. www.impawards.com.

What is G.I. Gin? http://forums.military.com.

ABOUT THE AUTHOR

Laura Van Dusen is a Colorado native and was raised in an 1890s Victorian home near Larkspur. She studied photography at Colorado Mountain College in Glenwood Springs, where she met her future husband, Tom.

After marriage, Tom and Laura lived in the Denver area for thirty-five years and raised two sons, Seth and Matt. They built a mountain cabin near Como, Colorado, in 1986 as a weekend retreat, and in 2010, Laura and Tom made that cabin their home.

Living in Park County rekindled Laura's interests in writing and Colorado history. Combining her interests, she began writing regularly for the *Park County Republican and Fairplay Flume* as a freelance correspondent two months after moving to the area. In October 2011, the first "Parked in the Past," a monthly feature exploring the history of Park County, was published in *The Flume*.

She is employed by the U.S. Forest Service in Fairplay, works seasonally at Fairplay's South Park City—a restored 1880s mining town—and is a member of the board of directors of the South Park National Heritage Area.

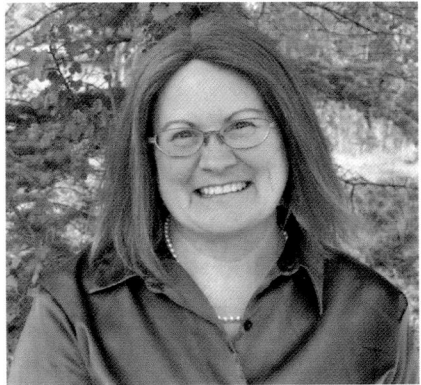

Visit us at
www.historypress.net
....
This title is also available as an e-book